GLOBAL ECONOMIC FORECAST 2010-2015

2010-2015

Recession Into Depression

Sheldon Filger

www.GlobalEconomicCrisis.com

Global Economic Forecast 2010-2015
Recession Into Depression

ISBN: 1449542263

As we peer into society's future, we — you and I, and our government — must avoid the impulse to live only for today, plundering for our own ease and convenience the precious resources of tomorrow. We cannot mortgage the material assets of our grandchildren without risking the loss also of their political and spiritual heritage. We want democracy to survive for all generations to come, not to become the insolvent phantom of tomorrow.

President Dwight D. Eisenhower
Farewell Address to the Nation; January 17, 1961

Contents

1
Executive Summary

Beginning with the collapse of the investment bank Lehman Brothers in September 2008, the world economy sank into a severe, synchronized recession. Prior to the disintegration of Lehman Brothers, most investment banks on Wall Street experienced severe solvency challenges, primarily related to the incendiary character of securitized subprime mortgages that they had transacted with. Thus, Bear Stearns had vanished as a major Wall Street presence, while Merrill Lynch would ultimately be absorbed by Bank of America simultaneously with the bankruptcy of Lehman Brothers.

The subprime debacle had already initiated a recession within the U.S. economy beginning in the latter part of 2007, however, it would not be until the aftermath of the Lehman Brothers implosion that this reality would be openly acknowledged by the U.S. government and its economic policymakers. Indeed, reality had caught up with the political decision makers, for in the wake of the Lehman Brothers bankruptcy the White House, the U.S. Treasury and the Federal Reserve openly conceded that the world was on the verge of a meltdown of the global financial system.

In February of 2008, the U.S. Congress approved an economic stimulus program involving tax rebates of more than $150 billion.

In the aftermath of the Lehman Brothers bankruptcy, Treasury Secretary Hank Paulson won approval from Congress for a $700 billion emergency appropriation to shore up the faltering U.S. financial system, what has since become known as TARP. This policy measure was replicated by governments throughout the world, especially in the United Kingdom and Eurozone. This was followed by a substantial stimulus measure enacted by the incoming Obama administration in the United States, totalling nearly $800 billion. Parallel with this step, other large economies also engaged in massive borrowing to fund economic stimulus programs, all based on the premise that government must substitute for the falloff in consumer demand that resulted from the onset of the worldwide financial crisis and credit crunch. As a proportion of GDP, China's $600 billion stimulus package is the largest direct government intervention in the economy that has occurred since the onset of the global economic crisis. All these steps have been justified as necessary to retard the free fall in employment numbers, reverse the trend and eventually restore economic growth and end what has become the most virulent synchronized global recession since the Great Depression of the 1930s.

In analyzing all the relevant economic data, GlobalEconomic-Crisis.com believes that the extraordinary and unprecedented interventions by sovereigns in the ongoing crisis have themselves become the most important factor in determining the longevity and character of the global recession, but in a manner neither anticipated nor planned by policymakers. On top of the already critical state of capital markets, credit flows, unemployment rates and private debt levels, it is our assessment that a looming sovereign debt crisis will occur within the next 18-24 months. This development will transform a synchronized global recession into a worldwide depression.

Global actors, especially developed as well as major developing economies, have in effect made a gamble involving their respective economic destinies. They are either engaged in public spending at levels far beyond their revenue generation capacity or are absorbing toxic private debt (in many cases both are occurring simultaneously) in the hope that these extreme policy measures will restore economic growth to levels that will sustain significantly higher rates of public debt servicing allocations, made necessary by those same policy measures. Our analysis leads to the conclusion that sovereigns throughout the world, in particular the United States and UK, will lose this gamble. Policymakers will then be left with several painful paths to select from, all of which will result in a sustained period of economic contraction and stagnation. While the temptation will exist among governments, economists, financial analysts and media commentators to avoid using the word "depression" as long as possible, the duration and severity of the global economic crisis will lead historians to conclude retrospectively that this period met the technical definition of an economic depression.

This report will present the data and macroeconomic trends that lead us to our conclusions regarding the likely duration and character of the global economic crisis. In addition, the geopolitical and social consequences of the global depression we are forecasting will be elaborated on, as these phenomena will also impact the duration and severity of the global economic crisis.

A summary of findings, as well as recommendations for policymakers in government, and decision makers within corporations and small businesses, will be presented in the section entitled, "conclusions and recommendations."

2
Setting the Stage:
The U.S. Recession of 2001

The traditional barometer for certifying a business cycle as recessionary in the United States is a period involving at least two consecutive quarters of negative GDP (Gross Domestic Product). Among economists and policymakers, a determination by the National Bureau of Economic Research that a significant decline in economic activity is occurring across the national economy, with the contraction from peak to trough lasting several months, has become the more functional definition of an economic recession.

Since the aftermath of the Great Depression of the 1930s and the massive economic mobilization required during the extraordinary circumstances of the Second World War, it has been accepted by economists and policymakers throughout the world that free market economies experience periods of economic contraction as intervals between periods of growth. Typically, postwar recessions are viewed as short or medium term economic phenomena, largely facilitated by distortions that occur during expansionary booms.

Different schools of thought have provided governments in free market economies with contradictory advice on how to respond to recessions. Generally, a mild recession is relatively short in time span, and is often concluded before radical government intervention can be fully enacted. Medium or severe recessions are often of sufficient duration for policymakers to intervene in the economy. In the United States, these policies have been increasingly influenced by ideology. In addition to the actions of the political echelon, central banks have becoming increasingly involved as independent actors, inserting monetary policy into the broad range of counter-cyclical responses to a business contraction.

In March 2001 the U.S. economy went into recession. The causes of the downturn were varied, however, a significant factor was the bursting of the dot-com asset bubble and the loss of half the equity value of the NASDAQ. In effect, speculation drove up the price of tech stocks to levels that seemed to ascend fundamental value, leading then chairman of the Federal Reserve, Alan Greenspan, to warn about "irrational exuberance."

Though the 2001 recession would be a mild one as compared with other postwar economic contractions, lasting eight months before GDP growth resumed, a number of factors led to policy interventions by both the government and Federal Reserve that were far more radical than typical policy responses to short-term periods of negative growth. The effect of these policy measures on the recession of 2001 are still debated, however their cumulative impact is highly relevant to the present global economic crisis. For that reason, it is important to review these factors.

In January 2001 George W. Bush was inaugurated as the 43rd president of the United States. He and his vice president, Dick Cheney, had a strong ideological commitment to Reagonomics, the name associated with the low tax and high deficit fiscal policies of the Reagan administration. Though at one time conservative economics meant frugal government, Reagonomics followed a different course. It believed in low taxation on high incomes, low government expenditures on social programs but a high level of public spending on the military and other national security activities. More a system of fiscal theology and financial dogmatism than coherent economic science, the adherents of Reagonomics were convinced that low taxes warranted large budgetary deficits in the short term, as this fiscal policy would unleash the creative energies of American capitalism, and ultimately lead to sustained high growth rates. It became an article of faith among the supporters of Reagonomics that eventually, even with a low tax rate, future high growth would lead to a balanced budget.

One of the first acts of the incoming Bush administration was to introduce a series of massive tax cuts that disproportionately benefited the nation's wealthiest citizens. The rationale used by President Bush was the recession of 2001, which officially began in March of that year. A major justification for this policy measure were the large federal budget surpluses that had accumulated in the latter part of the Clinton administration. Though these surpluses existed only because the substantial future liabilities for Social Security and Medicare are unfunded and off the books, on a relative scale the final years of President Clinton's administration did witness an improvement in the fiscal balance of the federal government. At the beginning of the Bush administration, it was assumed that even with significant tax cuts, the U.S. budget would remain in surplus (albeit only on paper) for many years into the future.

On September 11, 2001 the United States experienced a series of devastating terrorist attacks on its soil, perpetrated by Al-Qaeda. In addition to the geo-strategic consequences of this act, 9/11 was to have profound implications for the long-term stability of the U.S. economy. Though the recession of 2001 would officially end only weeks after 9/11, this act contributed to a perception that more radical steps were required to strengthen the nation's economy. Thus, in addition to the Bush tax cuts, the Federal Reserve, under the leadership of Alan Greenspan, instituted a wave of interest rate cuts that would eventually pump unprecedented levels of liquidity into the U.S. economy. Though in theory consumer price inflation remained under control during this period, in actuality the Fed's policies facilitated the creation of a new asset bubble in the United States, residential real estate. The Federal Reserve set its interest rate at 1.75% in December 2001, and would maintain a low interest rate policy for several years. It was during this period that unprecedented levels of price increases occurred among American homes throughout the nation, and especially in major cities and economic hubs.

Both during the Clinton and Bush administrations, deregulation of the financial industry became the norm. It was during the Clinton era that the provisions of the Glass-Steagall Act of 1933 pertaining to the separation of investment and commercial banking were annulled. This depression era legislation had been created in the wake of bank failures following the stock market crash of 1929. It aimed to protect the assets of commercial banks from the dangers inherent in financial speculation. The removal of this protection set the stage for the banking crisis that was to come.

The combination of banking and financial deregulation and the rapid increase in house prices led to the increasing securitization of home mortgages by Wall Street. These developments occurred simultaneously with the rapid expansion of a form of home finance that had traditionally been regarded as risky; subprime mortgages.

Federal Reserve monetary policies were pumping money into the mortgage market, while the government sponsored entities Fannie Mae and Freddie Mac were instituting policies that conformed to a Bush administration and congressional mandate to encourage home ownership. Individuals who previously had insufficient income to qualify for a home mortgage became candidates for subprime mortgages. The higher risk involved warranted an elevated interest rate, which translated into mortgage backed securities with a higher yield. Eventually, subprime mortgages would be sold by the initiating institutions to investment houses, who in turn sliced and diced these mortgages, combining them with near-prime and prime mortgages, supposedly reducing the risk through this admixture. These securitized mortgages would eventually be packaged and sold by Wall Street to investors throughout the world.

Another important economic trend that occurred in the United States in the wake of both the 2001 recession and 9/11 was the massive increase in military spending. In 2001, the U.S. defence budget was $307.8 billion. By 2008, the official defence budget had reached the figure of $494.4 billion (these figures are in constant dollars, adjusted for inflation), *excluding* the wars in Iraq and Afghanistan, which involved a supplementary military appropriation of $137 billion. When these additional figures are included, American military expenditures in 2008 exceeded $630 billion, representing a doubling of the defence budget in real terms in only seven years.

Though it is often stated by American political leaders that their nation is at war, in fact, aside from two low-intensity overseas counterinsurgency operations involving Al-Qaeda, a non-state actor with a few thousand adherents, the United States from a geo-strategic standpoint has enjoyed a near-peacetime security environment, especially with regard to major conventional threats. The more than doubling of the American defence budget, under the guise of the threat posed by a small guerrilla force, unsupported by a nation-state, in a period of only 7 years is unprecedented. Taking into account that this expansion of U.S. military allocations occurred without any reciprocal revenue enhancements, it became inevitable that severe strains on the fiscal posture of the United States would result.

The budget surplus of the Clinton administration was transformed into massive annual deficits by the Bush administration. The combination of revenue degradation, primarily through tax cuts weighing heavily on the highest income citizens and massive increases on military outlays, created what economists refer to as a structural deficit. As the name implies, a structural deficit is considered normative in government finances of a national economy. When the political elites accept the reality of structural deficits, the mechanisms for raising loans through the bond market and managing the growth of debt service payments as a core component of the budgetary pie become paramount.

The expanding fiscal imbalance that occurred during the Bush administration is important for understanding the dynamics of the current global economic crisis, and for the forecast that is contained in this report.

In essence, the aftermath of the 2001 recession and the 9/11 attacks in the United States resulted in a flurry of contradictory policy responses by the executive branch and Congress that would ultimately severely undermine the national economy. Asset bubbles were proliferating in the real estate sector, fed by the low funds rate of the Federal Reserve and policies enacted by the politicians. Deregulation of the financial industry was leading to high levels of securitization of subprime loans. Ideologically induced tax reductions were depressing the federal government's revenue generating capacity simultaneously with an unprecedented near-peacetime military build-up.

At the government level, fiscal discipline had broken down, while the private markets, in particular the financial industry, were running amok. The stage was being set for an economic implosion on a scale the world had not witnessed since the Great Depression.

3

The Emergence of
Derivatives In Global Finance

In the period following the recession of 2001, leading up to the financial crisis of 2008, investment vehicles of high complexity came to dominate the world of banking and finance. Commonly referred to as a derivatives, these transactions or contracts are based on an underlying asset. Derivatives are not new; futures contracts have been an important factor in global commerce for decades, particularly in relation to the purchase of commodities including oil, minerals and agricultural products such as wheat. What was novel in the middle of the first decade of the 21st century was the scale, diversification and complexity of these instruments. In earlier periods, various forms of derivatives had been employed as a hedge against risk, such as mitigating a possible future increase in energy prices. Increasingly, however, derivatives in the form of contracts and especially swaps became heavily relied on by large institutional investors and financial entities as speculative investment opportunities and large cash generators.

In the years leading up to the 2008 financial crisis, the notional value of derivatives of all types reached astronomical figures, for the most part without regulatory supervision equal to the systemic risks being created. Some investors and economists recognized the growing danger to the global economy being presented by the radical growth of derivatives. Warren Buffett, the billionaire investor, made an often quoted remark that derivatives were, in effect, "financial weapons of mass destruction."

One category of financial derivatives would come to play a dominating role in the global financial crisis of 2008; credit default swaps. A CDS is a derivative contract that in effect is a form of credit insurance. In essence, a CDS is structured as a guarantee by the issuer of payment to the purchaser of the instrument of credit reimbursement should the latter's investment vehicle or debtor default on payment. American International Group, more commonly known as AIG, the world's largest insurance company prior to the financial and economic crisis, became a major node of CDS derivative contracts. The London office of AIG spearheaded the insurance giant's credit default swap business. A large proportion of the firm's credit swaps involved mortgage backed securities and other forms of investment vehicles highly dependent on the American mortgage market, with a significant exposure to sub-prime home loans. These securitized investments were held by major financial institutions and investment houses throughout the world, especially in the United States, UK and Eurozone.

Though the CDS was an implicit guarantee of a mortgage backed security as well as other securitized investments, and AIG was primarily an insurance conglomerate, credit default swaps did not technically qualify as an insurance product. In actuality, this meant that AIG was not under any form of regulatory regime in the conduct of its CDS business arm operating out of its London office, in contrast with its other, more conventional insurance units. In addition, investment houses and financial institutions could purchase naked CDS contracts from AIG, meaning they were not the principal party owning the mortgage backed securitized investment.

What this meant in reality is that an investment bank or other financial institution could place a bet on the viability of a securitized investment held by a third party. If the securitized investment went into default, the owner of the CDS contract would collect on the value of the securitized asset, even though it was not the direct owner of the defaulting credit asset. Increasingly, derivative contracts such as the CDS vehicles being structured by AIG were instruments of speculation and casino-like gambling. In order for this model to work as a profitable arm for AIG, provision for reserves to cover payment on defaulting credit swaps had to be maintained at an exceedingly marginal level.

In the initial phase of this business development by AIG, the CDS model was seen as lucrative. Risks were deemed to be low, rationalizing in the eyes of AIG minimal provision for CDS payouts. This maximized the profitability of the business, as payments for CDS vehicles became a growing source of cash flow for AIG.

4

Global Financial Crisis of 2008

The trigger that unleashed the global financial crisis of 2008 was the puncturing of the U.S. residential real estate asset bubble. Over a ten year period ending in 2006, home prices in the United States more than doubled, far outpacing the official consumer price index and growth in real disposable income. At the beginning of President Bush's term of office in 2001, average U.S. home prices equaled roughly three times annual median individual income. That ratio climbed to 4.6 times average personal income in only five years.

With sluggish personal income growth occurring parallel with rapid home price inflation, American consumers were encouraged to use the equity growth of their personal residences as virtual ATM machines by refinancing and acquiring second mortgages. This proliferation of home equity loans injected nearly $5 trillion of credit generated liquidity into the global economy. In effect, the leveraging of the American consumer through home equity financing mechanisms was the basis of much of the measurable economic growth that occurred not only in the United States, but in other major economies benefiting from an expanding U.S. appetite for imported consumer goods.

The perception that U.S. house prices would escalate indefinitely facilitated a vast increase in the number of subprime mortgages that were granted to prospective homebuyers with marginal
incomes. In large part this was brought about through ARM, or
adjustable rate mortgages. Consumers were enticed into an ARM
loan based on an initial "teaser" rate set below market standards,
which would after an interval adjust to market rates, or in the case
of subprime mortgages, at levels above standard market rates and
substantially higher than the initial monthly payments. In the
wake of the financial and economic crisis, many details have
emerged indicating that mortgage brokers and banks in large
numbers of instances collaborated in selling subprime and ARM
mortgages to consumers with income levels inadequate for meeting their future obligations. Among examples cited are so-called
"NINJA loans," meaning "no income, no job, no assets."

The incentive model in effect at that time encouraged mortgage
brokers to sign up clients for loans irrespective of their income
levels, as the commissions would be paid regardless of whether or
not the mortgage eventually went into default. Under the new
model of loan securitization, lending institutions had little or no
incentive to ensure the quality of the borrower's financial capacity,
as the mortgages were rapidly bundled together and resold to Wall
Street. The investment industry securitized the mortgages and
marketed them to institutional and individual investors throughout the world, as noted previously. Typically, these mortgage
backed securities were presented as AAA grade, highly secure
investments. The ratings agencies largely failed to exercise the
necessary due diligence in assigning a rating that presented highly
risky securities as low risk investments.

In 2006 the rapid upward trajectory of U.S. residential real estate prices began to stagnate and then reverse course. As prices

began declining, some economists warned of the implications of this development for the wider economy. Home price declines became markedly worse in 2007, leading several economist to warn about the grave systemic dangers being posed to the global economy. Initially, these warnings were largely dismissed by policymakers and financial analysts, or downplayed.

In October 2005 Ben Bernanke, just prior to being nominated to succeed Alan Greenspan as chairman of the Federal Reserve, issued a statement claiming that the unprecedented rise in U.S. home prices did not constitute an asset bubble, and was based on sound economic fundamentals. Subsequently, in July 2007 Bernanke testified before a U.S. Senate panel on the economy, and presented the current view of the Fed regarding the vulnerability of the American economy to subprime mortgage defaults, which were becoming significantly more prolific.

Asked about the exposure of banks to subprime credit, Bernanke told the Senate panel, "some estimates are in the order of between $50 billion and $100 billion of losses associated with subprime credit problems."

Believing that the maximum risk posed to the American economy due to subprime credit problems did not exceed $100 billion, a small fraction of total U.S household net worth, the Federal Reserve suggested, at worst, that housing contraction would be a drag on projected economic growth, but not a trapdoor leading to recession. Chairman Bernanke's cautiously optimistic Senate testimony is symptomatic of a failure of imagination and intellectual capacity by key Washington decision makers, impeding their ability to fully comprehend the financial and economic storm that was about to be unleashed. It was only when the impact of the subprime meltdown became undeniable that policymakers began to appreciate the seriousness of the situation. By then, it was too late to prevent a virtual meltdown of the global financial order.

In 2008 the cascading forces of house price deflation, financial deregulation and economic globalization collided, resulting in a financial crisis that steadily grew worse as the year progressed. As the U.S. financial system encountered increasing levels of balance sheet toxicity due to the erosion in value of mortgage backed securities, the political echelon and the Federal Reserve exhibited a growing level of disarray, resulting in a series of erratic, ad hoc and insufficient policy responses, with poor or non-existing coordination.

Bear Stearns, one of the flagship Wall Street investment banks, with a long history that included survival of the Great Depression, had been one of the principal innovators of securitization. The mounting losses from toxic investments based on mortgage backed securities created a high level of exposure for Bear Stearns, severely eroding its liquidity. In March of 2008 the firm entered into a death spiral, forcing the Federal Reserve and U.S. Treasury to cobble together a rescue operation. What is significant with the Bear Stearns situation in 2008 is not only its historical role as the first major investment bank to collapse in the wake of the subprime mortgage crisis; the extraordinary government intervention created a new doctrine that has come to dominate all future policy responses by sovereigns in confronting the rapidly escalating financial crisis: the concept of "too big to fail."

The underlying principle of the "too big to fail" doctrine is that in exceptional cases, several private companies operating in the financial field have become so large, their demise would threaten the very foundation of the national and global financial system. In other words, should a company reach a threshold of aggregate size deemed "too big to fail," its liquidation would then pose an unacceptable systemic risk and would require all necessary public interventions, including taxpayer bailouts, to prevent bankruptcy. Initially, even the authors of this doctrine were awkward with its justification, as it clearly contradicted the ethos of moral hazard, and the essential philosophy of free market capitalism, in which business failure is seen as the inherent risk of entrepreneurship. In the past, bankruptcy was viewed as the "creative destruction" of modern capitalism, enabling more successful business models to replace failure, in effect, the Darwinian principle of "survival of the fittest." However, as the financial crisis escalated, the power structures in the United States, and eventually in other major free market economies, would increasingly abandon adherence to principles and concepts that had served as the bedrock of modern capitalism since its emergence with the advent of industrialization.

In January 2007 the share price of Bear Stearns had reached a peak of $172. On March 16, 2008 Fed Chairman Bernanke brokered a deal whereby Bear Stearns was absorbed by JP Morgan Chase, initially at a mere $2 per share; that figure was subsequently increased to $10 per share in response to adverse reaction from investors, still signifying the virtual annihilation of shareholder equity. The Federal Reserve assumed the risk of Bear Stearns toxic assets through provision of a $29 billion non-recourse loan to JP Morgan Chase. This staggering level of potential taxpayer liability as a backstop to failure by a major Wall Street firm also marked an important precedent in how far Washington policymakers were prepared to go in making the public purse the ultimate firewall for the increasingly fragile Wall Street firms and major banks.

Prior to the worsening situation on Wall Street, the U.S. Congress had already enacted the Economic Stimulus Act of 2008, seen as a fiscal policy measure aimed at forestalling a possible recession. This stimulus package provided $152 billion in tax rebates, the aim being to facilitate higher consumer spending and forestall GDP quarterly contraction. At the time that Congress approved the Economic Stimulus Act of 2008, the federal government already had a significant structural deficit. The stimulus package more than doubled the previous year's deficit, raising the anticipated fiscal imbalance in 2008 to more than $400 billion.

In the wake of the virtual disappearance of Bear Stearns and increasingly negative economic news, government spokespersons and key decision makers attempted to reassure the American public during the summer of 2008 that America's financial system was fundamentally sound, and that the significant but ad hoc steps taken by the Federal Reserve and U.S. Treasury, in conjunction with the Bush administration's fiscal stimulus measures, would contain the negative impact of the subprime meltdown on the wider U.S. economy. However, in September of 2008, these reassurances were blown apart by the near disintegration of the global financial system.

Prior to the fiscal Armageddon that exploded in September, the global economy was already under severe strain as a result of a massive spike in petroleum prices. The emergence of China and India as major consumers of oil added a whole new layer of price pressure on energy commodities. The price of a barrel of oil reached a peak level in excess of $140 a barrel during the summer of 2008. Though the global financial crisis and resulting synchronized recession would just as spectacularly deflate oil prices, the short term elevation in energy prices ensured that the global economy would be under immense strain. This heightened its vulnerability to a major global financial shock.

The deteriorating housing market in the United States had a calamitous effect on Fannie Mae and Freddie Mac, the two government sponsored but privately held entities that collectively accounted for half of the $12 trillion of outstanding U.S. household mortgages. They were placed under the auspices of the Federal Housing Finance Agency (FHFA) on September 7, 2008 and provided with tens of billions of dollars of taxpayer support to prevent their imminent bankruptcy.

On September 15, the accumulation of toxic debt and illiquidity came to a head when Lehman Brothers filed for Chapter 11 bankruptcy. The U.S. Treasury and Federal Reserve made a decision to allow Lehman Brothers to fold, assuming its demise would not pose a systemic risk to the global financial system. In the same timeframe that policymakers were deliberating in Washington over the fate of Lehman Brothers, different conclusions were reached with regards to Merrill Lynch and AIG. In the case of the former, the Fed and Treasury cobbled together a deal whereby Bank of America bought Merrill Lynch, with considerable taxpayer support. Without the deal, Merrill Lynch faced financial liquidation. AIG was also on the verge of bankruptcy, due solely to the exposure of its CDS operations. Treasury Secretary Paulson stated that AIG was so large a factor in the global financial system, its business liquidation could not be allowed to occur, regardless of the subsidies required to keep it afloat. Through the middle of 2009, the U.S. government would inject in excess of $180 billion into AIG.

The calculation made by Bernanke and Paulson was apparently that moral hazard required that not all investment banking and financial firms be defined as being "too big to fail." Lehman Brothers was deemed expendable, the belief being that the extraordinary measures taken to save AIG and Merrill Lynch were sufficient to weather the storm connected with a Lehman Brothers collapse. As with so much else about the Fed and Treasury Department in terms of assessing the extent of the fast developing crisis, they underestimated the destructive forces that had been unleashed. When Lehman Brothers imploded, its debris virtually froze the entire global interbank lending mechanism, and brought the flow of credit to a virtual standstill.

An immediate consequence of the disintegration of Lehman Brothers was the accelerating rise in the LIBOR and Ted Spreads, reflecting frozen global credit markets saturated with counterparty risk aversion. Money market funds were being rapidly depleted, creating a state of panic among central bankers and treasury officials worldwide. A consensus quickly evolved among policy-makers that only the massive intervention of sovereigns, involving vast deficit expenditures to backstop major financial institutions, would prevent a global financial meltdown and economic depression.

In the crisis atmosphere that prevailed after the bankruptcy filing of Lehman Brothers, U.S. Treasury Secretary Paulson and Federal Reserve Chairman Bernanke decided to end their ad hoc responses to the worsening financial crisis, and formulate a holistic approach. They presented to Congress an urgent request for rapid passage of funding for the Troubled Asset Relief Program, commonly referred to as TARP. This legislation required an emergency appropriation of $700 billion, a figure that would be added to the national debt. The initial purpose, as proposed by Paulson, was to use the TARP funds to buy toxic assets sitting on the balance sheets of major banks, in the process facilitating their ability to resurrect normal patters of credit flow to businesses and consumers. After passage of the TARP legislation, however, Paulson changed the original plan he had proposed, and in lieu of purchasing troubled assets, Treasury took an equity stake in major banks, providing a direct infusion of capital into these institutions.

In the weeks following the elimination of Lehman Brothers, it became increasingly clear to economists, financial analysts and policymakers that the world had entered the worst global economic crisis since the Great Depression of the 1930s. A negative feedback loop ensured that the financial catastrophe sparked by the sub-prime mortgage meltdown in the United States would impose a severe cost to the economies of major developed and developing nations. A lack of counterparty confidence was leading to a run on the global banking system, while asset classes in virtually every category were undergoing deleveraging. Consumption was in free fall, contributing to a synchronized global recession.

The global financial crisis of 2008 had created a context which made it inevitable that decision makers in major economies would formulate policy responses that were unprecedented in their scope, scale and radical character.

5

Policymakers Respond to the Global Economic Crisis

Two parallel paths were pursued by sovereigns in response to the severe global recession. There was universal recognition that the financial system had to be stabilized and restored to health, if economies were to return to stable growth. Simultaneously with salvaging the banking systems that were in dire straits in many major economies, there was a wide consensus that sovereigns would need to go into debt and fund massive economic stimulus programs. The concern was that an extended recession would lead to further erosion in the market value of collateral debt obligations and other assets sitting on the balance sheets of many major financial institutions. In essence, the problems of the financial and economic sectors, the latter being what is frequently referred to as the "real economy," were interlinked to such an extent that policy measures had to be directed at both aspects or else be rendered ineffective.

The subprime mortgage meltdown in the United States had far-reaching consequences for financial institutions and governments across the globe. The United Kingdom's banking sector was especially vulnerable, given its high exposure to securities based on American residential mortgages.

The British bank Northern Rock, one of the five largest mortgage lenders in the United Kingdom, became the first financial
institution in that country to suffer critical liquidity problems.
After several successive injections of liquidity into Northern Rock
by the Bank of England, and following failed attempts to sell the
bank to private investors, the British government decided in
February 2009 to nationalize the bank. This was only the beginning
of a massive taxpayer supported bailout of the UK banking system
undertaken by Prime Minister Gordon Brown, who had previously
served as Chancellor of the Exchequer under his predecessor,
Prime Minister Tony Blair. Subsequently, the Royal Bank of
Scotland and Lloyds TSB would receive recapitalization from the
British taxpayer, potentially as high as 60% of the former and 40%
of the latter in terms of an equity stake.

In the wake of the massive borrowing spree engaged in by
Prime Minister Brown and his Chancellor of the Exchequer,
Alistair Darling, to prop of the British banking system, there was
much initial praise for their policy response to the crisis. Gordon
Brown even took credit for helping to stabilize the global financial
system, boasting in a speech that he had "saved the world."

In January 2009, however, a confidential meeting was con-
ducted at 10 Downing Street involving Prime Minister Brown,
Financial Services Authority chairman Lord Turner and Bank of
England governor Mervyn King. The purpose of the meeting was
to discuss a report prepared by financial analysts at the Royal Bank
of Scotland entitled, "Living on a Prayer." The report concluded
that UK banks were "technically insolvent, " indicating that
despite the Brown government's expenditure of nearly $400 billion
to prop up British banks impacted by the global financial and
economic crisis, this unprecedented level of taxpayer support had
almost entirely failed to curtail the repercussions of the credit

crunch. Substantial additional public injections of capital would be required, adding further strains to Britain's growing fiscal imbalance.

The combined UK expenditures for salvaging the nation's financial sector and coping with the recession that had severely impacted the economy, created unprecedented budgetary strains. Estimates for the 2009 fiscal year projected a deficit potentially in excess of $140 billion; for 2008 the deficit was £78 billion, representing 5.4% of the UK's GDP.

As the economic free fall resulting from the severe damage to the global financial system took on the character of a virulent, synchronized global recession, the nations making up the G20, representing the largest economic powers in the world, initiated a wide range of fiscal and monetary responses to the global economic and financial crisis. This typically took the form of historically low interest rate policies adopted by the central banks, combined with massive sovereign borrowing to fund expansive bailouts of the financial sector and economic stimulus packages to stem the rapid growth in unemployment. In the case of the nations comprising the Eurozone, a single entity, the European Central Bank (ECB) was responsible for monetary policy in all 16 countries that made up the currency union. As Europe sank into its worst post-World War II recession, the ECB reduced its funds rate to 1%.

Germany adapted a $40 billion economic stimulus package in November 2008, as its export-driven economy felt the weight of trade contraction that followed in the aftermath of the financial crisis. The primary intervention by the German government was in shoring up its financial sector. A massive commitment of up to $514.4 billion was undertaken by the political echelon as a three-year guarantee for all interbank lending, with an additional $100 billion in direct equity injections set aside for troubled banks.

France approved a $34 billion stimulus package, with similar budgetary initiatives also undertaken by other major European economies, as well as in Japan, Canada and Australia. As recognition grew that the aftermath of the financial implosion of 2008 had resulted in a severe global economic crisis, many national economies; large, medium and small, dug into the public purse to counteract the effects of rising unemployment.

As the crisis evolved, smaller economies that had been thriving in an environment of financial globalization and deregulation were impacted in uniquely severe way. Singapore suffered significant GDP contraction at the onset of the global economic crisis, while other Asian economies that were export dependent incurred similar afflictions. Ireland's economy underwent free fall contraction, while Eastern Europe and Russia felt the full impact of a synchronized global recession. However, Iceland probably represented, on a per capita basis, the most catastrophic immediate impact resulting from the 2008 financial tsunami.

Iceland once had a reputation for hardworking fishermen, and financial thriftiness. Its budgets were usually balanced or in surplus, and its banking sector was tightly regulated. However, a new generation of political and financial elites brought in an ideology of free market supremacy, leading to unrestrained banking and financial deregulation. Extreme financial engineering created a business model for Iceland's banking sector that led these institutions to take on a high level of short-term debt, while offering above-market interest rates to entice new bank depositors from overseas. Iceland's banks eventually accrued more depositors outside of Iceland, especially the United Kingdom, when the global financial crisis exploded during 2008.

Iceland's three largest banks became insolvent as the credit crunch pinched their access to short-term financing while simultaneously overseas depositors began a run on those banks. This resulted in a panicky Icelandic government being forced to place in receivership and thus nationalize Glitnir Bank, Landsbanki and Kaupthing, the latter being the nation's largest bank. The potential liabilities of these banks exceeded the entire GDP of Iceland by a multiple of ten, forcing the government to seek emergency financial aid from the International Monetary Fund (IMF) as the country's currency, the krona, went into free fall collapse.

The financial catastrophe that engulfed Iceland inflicted crippling damage to her economy and brought about a severe political crisis that was unprecedented in her history. Prime Minister Geir Haarde was forced to resign and call early elections, as the world witnessed how an entire country can undergo apocalyptic levels of economic carnage due to the collapse of its banking sector.

It would, however, be the world's first and third largest economies, the United States and China respectively, where the most important policy responses to the global crisis were undertaken. In the U.S., the epicentre and to a decisive degree the facilitator of the crisis, policy decisions were complicated by the political transition occurring simultaneously with the Lehman Brothers bankruptcy and its catastrophic aftermath. The controversial TARP program was deliberated on in Congress in the final weeks of the 2008 presidential campaign, requiring the Republican and Democratic nominees, Senators John McCain and Barack Obama, to engage in uncharacteristic cooperation in an effort to achieve bipartisan support for Treasury Secretary Paulson's Wall Street bailout package.

The level of coordination that presidential candidate Barack Obama had with the lame duck Bush administration regarding the financial crisis created the contextual foundation for a high degree of policy continuity after his inauguration as America's 44th president. Obama selected as Director of the White House's National Economic Council, Larry Summers, who had served as Treasury Secretary under President Bill Clinton and had been an advocate of financial deregulation. President Obama also picked Timothy Geithner, president of the New York Federal Reserve Bank, to be his Treasury Secretary. In August of 2009 Obama reappointed Ben Bernanke to a second term as chairman of the Federal Reserve.

The top priority of the Obama administration during its first weeks in office was passage of its economic stimulus package. The American Recovery and Reinvestment Act of 2009 was enacted by Congress in February 2009, requiring an appropriation of $787 billion. This entire sum would be added to the national debt and annual deficits. In sheer fiscal terms, the Obama stimulus package was the largest in history, and equalled approximately 5.6% of America's GDP. President Obama maintained that without the stimulus spending, the unemployment rate would exceed 8.5%. However, by the summer of 2009, despite the stimulus package, the U.S. unemployment rate had already reached a figure of 9.5%, according to the Labor Department.

Another immediate concern that was addressed by the Obama administration was the dismal state of the domestic automobile manufacturing industry. Though the problems afflicting Ford, General Motors and Chrysler were longstanding, the synchronized global recession was leading to demand destruction on an unprecedented scale. Major automobile manufacturers, not only in the United States but throughout the world, were severely impacted by both the economic downturn and vast overcapacity. Global car manufacturing capacity exceeded 90 million units annually, while consumer demand had dropped to just above 50 million car purchases per year. GM and Chrysler were especially vulnerable to the contraction in the auto industry, placing both firms on the verge of bankruptcy. Labor unions and their political supporters pressured the Obama administration to bailout the auto industry, basing much of their case on the vast levels of taxpayer support already provided to Wall Street. Ultimately, the Obama administration adopted a compromise approach. GM and Chrysler were both required to enter the Chapter 11 bankruptcy process, emerging with much of their liabilities eradicated. Government financial assistance was provided to both companies, enabling them to remain in business, though with a much reduced workforce. In effect, the U.S. government became the majority owner of the reorganized General Motors, a form of nationalization in reality if not in name. When GM has shed its payroll to planned levels, it will be employing a workforce that has been reduced by 92% from the peak levels it had during the 1950s. The cost to U.S. taxpayers for the subsidized downsizing of the Detroit automakers exceeded $30 billion by mid-2009; some estimates project that this figure may eventually reach $100 billion.

It was the ongoing banking crisis, however, that remained the most severe challenge for the Obama presidency. The unpopularity of the $700 billion TARP program created a high degree of reluctance on the part the Obama administration to inject much more taxpayer money into the banking system. However, the state of America's banks remained precarious. Initially, it would be left to the Federal Reserve to insert major policy interventions into the bank rescue efforts, making use of its vast power and political independence. Surviving Wall Street firms, in particular Goldman Sachs, were able to transform themselves into bank holding companies, making them eligible for taxpayer-subsidized credit to ensure their liquidity. As the creator of the nation's money supply, the Fed made use of its literal and electronic printing press to create money to purchase risky assets from troubled financial institutions and to provide substantial credit lines, as with the case of AIG. The balance sheet of the Federal Reserve mushroomed to over $2 trillion, inclusive of toxic assets from banks and U.S. Treasuries.

Despite the measures implemented by the Fed, U.S. banks remained in poor condition, with their balance sheets overloaded with troubled assets. Many economists felt that a large section of the U.S. banking sector, including several of its largest institutions, were functionally insolvent. There was a consensus by many leading analysts that the U.S. government would be required to nationalize these banks temporarily, close those that could not be saved, then recapitalize those that could be salvaged, in the process purging them of their toxic assets. It was estimated that this process would cost the taxpayers an additional $2 trillion. A similar process had occurred in Sweden during its banking crisis in the 1990s, though on a much smaller scale. The Swedish experience, however, did provide a model for temporary nationalization as a cleansing process for troubled banks, ultimately leading to their resale as viable entities to the private sector.

President Obama and his principal economic advisors chose not to consider nationalization as a policy option for coping with the nation's banking crisis. Instead, they adopted a series of improvised steps, predicated on the belief that the economic stimulus package would eventually translate into higher asset valuations for the banking system's balance sheets.

The major initiative for addressing the toxic assets was announced by the Obama administration in March 2009. Dubbed the Public-Private Investment Program for Legacy Assets, it involved the participation of the Treasury Department, Federal Reserve and Federal Deposit Insurance Corporation (FDIC). The program involved taxpayer money, potentially up to $100 billion from the TARP program, being made available in partnership with capital from private investors, to purchase troubled assets from banks. In theory, risks and rewards would be shared between public and private stakeholders. However, the program encountered significant criticism, not the least being that banks would be reluctant to sell their assets at fair market value, which would represent a substantial loss. The complex matter of price discovery in determining the real value of the toxic assets would remain a vexatious obstacle to any effort to attract private money as a means for resolving the troubled assets predicament.

With no immediate solution to the banking crisis in sight, though the threat of a quick financial meltdown averted by massive sovereign injection of taxpayer money into the global financial system, Treasury Secretary Geithner embarked on a new stratagem for convincing markets and investors that the American banking system was on a stable recovery mode and fundamentally solvent. The banking stress tests, completed in the spring of 2009, were supposed to reveal how well the major American banks could weather a severe recession, under the most challenging economic circumstances. According to Geithner, at most, some of the banks would require $75 billion in additional capital, all of which could be raised from private investors. In essence, the U.S. government was proclaiming that the nation's banking system was solvent with strong capitalization, only six months after the $700 billion TARP bailout and near implosion of the global financial system. Critics pointed out several flaws with the modeling used by the Treasury Department in the execution of its stress tests. The exposure of several of the large intuitions to toxic assets and derivatives was not properly evaluated. "Worst case" unemployment scenarios were unrealistic, and would in fact be surpassed by the summer of

2009. In essence, it appeared that the government stress test was more of a public relations exercise than a comprehensive examination of the fiscal health of the primary banking organizations in the United States.

In addition to the actions undertaken by the administration, Congress exerted its own influence in an effort to construct a better picture of the American banking system than reality warranted. Under intense pressure from politicians, the Financial Accounting Standards Board (FASB), which establishes generally accepted accounting practices, was forced to modify its mark to market requirement to a mark to model rule. This accounting rule change allowed troubled banks to set an inflated valuation on their toxic assets. The implication of this balance sheet transformation meant that less reserves had to be set aside for loan loss provision. This change, along with other unique benefits made available to banks through the various government bailout efforts, allowed several major financial intuitions that had incurred large losses in 2008 to declare a profit for Q1 of 2009.

In practice, U.S. policymakers were replicating the response of Japanese decision makers to their nation's banking crisis that resulted from the collapse of real estate and equity assets in their economy in the 1990s. Tokyo decided against a purgative approach towards its insolvent banks, choosing instead to keep them on a form of fiscal life support, leading to the popular reference to these financial institutions as "zombie banks." The Japanese political establishment did spend heavily on economic stimulus programs to counteract the effects of the resulting severe recession; these policy responses were, for the most part, unsuccessful. The failure of Japanese economic and fiscal policies resulted in a prolonged period of stagnation that followed the nation's economic downturn. This period, which endured for more than a decade, is described by economists as an L shaped recession, meaning after a major economic downturn, growth is sluggish or nonexistent for an extended period of time.

On the surface, the Obama administration's policy measures appeared to have had a moderating influence on the most immediate dangers that resulted from the Lehman Brothers collapse. The free fall contraction in U.S. GDP appeared to have abated; it was -6.4% in Q1 of 2009 but had officially receded to only -1% in Q2. However, U.S. government spending had increased by 10.9% in Q2 versus a decrease of 4.3% in Q1. In actuality, massive borrowing and spending by the federal government was compensating for a substantial drop in consumer spending. While on paper this policy response was levelling off the economic downturn in America, this was being achieved at a vast increase in the budgetary deficit and national debt.

In 2007 the U.S. budget deficit was $163 billion; it more than doubled in 2008, reaching $455 billion, primarily due to tax rebates flowing from that fiscal year's economic stimulus package, as described previously. In 2009, however, the federal government's annual deficit had reached $1.6 trillion, a figure that would have been even higher had the Obama administration not backed out of its previous allocation of hundreds of billions of dollars for further stabilization of the banking system and provision for additional FDIC funds to cope with an expected rise in bank failures.

In 2000 the official gross national debt of the United States federal government was $5.6 trillion. By the summer of 2009, the national debt had exceeded $11.7 trillion, representing a doubling of that figure in only nine years, at a time of low inflation. Over the same period the nominal GDP of the U.S. had grown from $10 trillion to $14 trillion. In other words, economic growth lagged significantly behind the increase in the national debt, in effect doubling the debt to GDP ratio. By 2009, America's official national debt to GDP ratio had exceeded 80%.

In the summer of 2009, the Congressional Budget Office released a revised ten year forecast on the cumulative fiscal deficit of the U.S. government. The previous CBO estimate had forecast a cumulative deficit of $7 trillion; the revised projection was for a $9 trillion federal deficit over the next decade.

The rising government deficits in the United States and Eurozone, while justified by policymakers as vital for saving the world from another Great Depression, began creating growing concern among some decision makers. At the G7 summit in Rome of finance ministers, held in February 2009, a voice of caution was raised regarding the unprecedented pump-priming being undertaken by sovereigns. The German Finance ministers, Peer Steinbrueck, warned his colleagues that there was a need to prepare an "exit strategy" to address the massive influx of liquidity into the global financial system. German policymakers would reflect a more fiscally conservative outlook on the economic and financial crisis than their counterparts in the U.S. and UK, emphasizing the danger of creating new asset bubbles and laying the groundwork for high rates of inflation. In contrast, U.S. and UK decision makers felt that Germany should have joined them in engaging in far more expansive stimulus packages.

Yet, as the U.S. deficit soared along with long-term projections for the national debt, American economic policymakers began to engage in a duality of public commentary; continuing to insist that the growing public indebtedness was necessary in the short-term, but proclaiming that the Obama administration was committed to reducing the nation's fiscal imbalance in the long-term. Fed Chairman Bernanke began adopting the language of the German finance minister, publicly stating the need for an exit strategy by the Federal Reserve from its loose monetary policies, while simultaneously engaging in unprecedented quantitative easing and purchasing of public debt instruments and private assets.

In large part, the public commitment to a restoration of fiscal balance engaged in by key U.S. economic decision makers in the government was necessitated by a need to assuage the growing anxiety among America's major foreign creditors, in particular China. Chinese public officials, including President Hu Jintao, began stating on the public record their unease at the accelerating level of public indebtedness of the United States, and the threat this fiscal reality posed for their substantial investment in U.S. government debt instruments.

China, as the world's third largest economy at the onset of the crisis and principal purchaser of U.S. Treasuries, was not immune to severe consequences from the evolving global economic downturn. The financial meltdown of 2008 had precipitated a free fall contraction in global trade, creating grave ramifications for China's export-based economy. The nation's high growth levels had in large part been facilitated by the American consumer. With consumers in the United States and Europe undergoing deleveraging and suffering high rates of unemployment, demand for Chinese exports declined precipitously. Official statistics revealed that in July 2009 Beijing's exports had decreased by 23% from July of 2008.

Recognizing the implications of the global economic crisis for their export-based economic model, Beijing undertook a massive stimulus program, announced in March 2009. It involved spending 4 trillion yuan, equivalent to $586 billion at the prevailing exchange rate, the second largest such package after the U.S. in nominal terms. However, with a GDP of $4 trillion versus $14 trillion for the United States, the Chinese stimulus spending package was by far the largest in the world, in terms of its proportion to GDP; 14.6% versus 5.6% in the U.S.

The priority for China's political leadership was the maintenance of social stability. The dynamics of the Chinese economy function in a very different manner from major developed economies; a growth rate in excess of 6% is required in order to maintain stable employment, compared with 2.5% in the United States. The wave of factory closures resulting from the falloff in export orders was estimated to have cost 25 million migrant Chinese workers their jobs by the spring of 2009. With social tensions and ethnic unrest already a growing concern for Beijing, and with ample foreign exchange reserves available to the treasury, the Chinese government calculated it would be strategically advisable to make a major fiscal investment in the economy, the goal being to retard a major rise in the nation's unemployment rate.

While Beijing's sizeable economic stimulus package was established to address internal Chinese priorities, major economic actors, including developed and developing economies and multinational corporations, looked to China to play the primary role in counteracting the global recession. When, despite the double digit decline in Chinese exports, the authorities were able to project a growth rate in the national economy for between 7 and 8% in 2009, many economists and financial analysts pointed to this statistical calculation as evidence that the global economy was recovering from the synchronized recession that had resulted from the financial crisis of 2008. The Chinese quarterly measurements of GDP growth were the primary basis for the World Bank moderating its projection on global economic contraction in 2009, the first year it was reporting worldwide negative economic growth.

However, beyond a superficial perusal of official government statistics, there appeared to some a very dangerous side to China's economic stimulus spending. As dictated by the authorities in Beijing, staggering amounts of cash were pumped into the economy. To illustrate the flow of capital being stimulated by China's fiscal policy measures, in the first half of 2009 Chinese banks loaned $1 trillion. By way of comparison, in all of 2008 only $600 billion was provided to borrowers by China's banks and financial institutions. With credit now flowing so free and easy towards Chinese companies, in many instances they responded by engaging in rash speculation, rather than with enhancing production and employment. In effect, the corporate sector in China utilized the stimulus money doled out by the government to engage in speculation involving commodities, real estate and equities. As an example, there were cases involving Chinese companies that had established dedicated departments focussed on the sole task of speculating with the easy credit being offered at Beijing's insistence by China's banks, in lieu of the intricacies of marketing, sales, R & D and production.

Easy credit leading to speculation in China's real estate and equity markets created a rising level of concern by some observers and decision makers within the Chinese political echelon that asset bubbles might result from the pumping of excess liquidity into the national economy. In addition, as with deficit-driven stimulus spending elsewhere, China's fiscal response to the economic crisis was viewed by Beijing as a stop-gap measure, its leadership recognizing that this policy response to the global economic crisis could not be continued indefinitely. As with other major economies engaged in similar policy actions, economic policymakers were debating over the timing of an exit strategy, and the sustainability of a robust economic recovery once the pump-priming was curtailed.

6
2010-2011: Illusory Recovery Undermined By Sovereign Debt

A transitional period will follow the massive sovereign interventions in the global financial system and economy that
were initiated by policymakers in 2009. This period we foresee
enduring for the next 18-24 months, concluding with a catastrophic
debt crisis that will paralyse the ability of sovereign governments
to continue massive borrowing in support of financial system
bailouts and economic stimulus spending. This will mark the next
stage of the global economic crisis, which will be dealt with in the
following chapter of this report.

Much of 2010 will be characterized by a deceptive calming of
the crisis. Massive borrowing engaged in by governments across
the globe, especially in the United States, will be recorded as GDP
growth, creating the impression that the economy has slipped out
of recession, and is beginning a period of recovery and tentative
growth. There will be an attempt by political actors and media
commentators to spin the debt-induced quarterly economic indicators as concrete evidence that the crisis is "over" and normal
consumer spending patterns and demand creation can resume.
However, the official statistical measurements on economic growth
will not accurately gauge the lingering impact of a severely dam-

aged financial system in the United States, UK and the Eurozone. Businesses that had laid off employees to pare costs and remain competitive amid lower production norms, will be reluctant to begin the process of rehiring. The continuing credit crunch and weak demand will facilitate an increase in business and personal bankruptcies in many major economies. These trends, reinforcing each other, will ensure that unemployment continues to increase, or at best stabilize at historically high numbers.

Unemployment in advanced economies that make up the bulk of global consumer demand will exacerbate two indicators that are critical metrics for gauging the future trajectory of the crisis. Economies that depend on a large export sector, in particular China, Japan and Germany, will be severely impacted. This will contribute to fiscal and economic challenges that will eventually reverse initial quarterly indicators that suggest that these countries have ended their recessions. In the U.S. and UK, the curtailment in consumer purchasing power resulting from employment attenuation will increase the level of toxic assets on the balance sheets of large numbers of American and British banks, eventually precipitating a new and potentially more dangerous phase of the banking crisis.

To put the projected decline in consumer spending, especially in the United States, in its proper context, it is instructive to review the centrality of consumer spending as the driver of economic growth. From 2000 until the onset of the recession in 2007, personal spending by American consumers accounted for 77% of GDP growth in the United States. This development was based almost entirely on exploding household debt in the U.S. and the collapse of personal savings by American consumers. By the beginning of the recession in 2007, the level of household debt in the U.S. had reached $13.8 trillion, equal to nearly 140% of disposable income, an historic high. Personal savings had declined to a net negative of nearly one percent.

The global financial and economic crisis has reversed these trends. A process of massive deleveraging by American consumers began with the onset of the recession, and will continue to gain momentum throughout 2010-2011. Personal savings rates will again be in positive territory, hovering at 5% or higher as a proportion of disposable income. Taking into account that the rise in unemployment and other economic factors have exerted anti-inflationary pressures on U.S. wages, there will be no counter-weight in terms of individual income enhancement to offset the falloff in consumer spending that will result from the deleveraging and higher savings rates that will increasingly characterize the behaviour of the American consumer.

The premise underlying deficit driven economic stimulus programs is based on the theories of the Great Depression era economist Maynard Keynes, who advocated public borrowing and spending in times of an economic contraction as a counter-cyclical policy measure. In essence, it is centered on the belief that rising unemployment reduces household spending in the economy; an increase in government spending on a temporary basis can substitute for the falloff in personal consumption, thus limiting the negative repercussions of a severe economic recession.

However, the $787 billion Obama stimulus package, designed to replace consumer demand eliminated by rising unemployment in the United States, is insufficient to redress the long-term implications of the deleveraging underway among American households. That trend, and a much higher than anticipated unemployment rate, will reduce the capacity of the administration's stimulus package to generate a return to GDP growth at a level sufficient to reduce joblessness and restore consumer confidence.

As the combination of reduced debt-to-income levels by American consumers and rising unemployment undermines the efficacy of the Obama stimulus program, there will be pressure to initiate a supplemental stimulus appropriation in 2010. Fearful of adding to the national debt and arousing concern in the bond markets, the political leadership in Washington is likely to try short-term improvisations as a means of improving quarterly economic results in key categories, hoping to forestall the need for another expenditure of hundreds of billions of dollars. An example of such a policy response was the "cash for clunkers" program implemented during the summer of 2009, which paid American consumers up to $4,500 to replace an older vehicle with a new car. In the short-run, this program stimulated purchases of automobiles. However, such a program is no different than the rebates that had been offered by major automobile manufacturers in the United States for many years, which had proven not to be a long-term strategic solution to the systemic problems in that industry. Ultimately, the political echelon and its economic advisors will recognize that such Band-Aid approaches only push forward consumer demand from a later quarter, with little or no actual impact on sustained economic growth.

An additional economic stimulus appropriation in 2010, combined with a continuing attrition in tax receipts from individuals and corporations, will impose further stress on the federal government's annual budget. The 2010 deficit, likely to exceed $1.5 trillion dollars, will send a message to sovereign creditors and the bond market that the United States is trapped in a long-term structural mega-deficit, with the gap of expenditures over revenue well in excess of a trillion dollars per annum for at least the next decade. There will be increasing doubt among America's creditors as to the sustainability of her structural mega-deficits, reflected in a rising degree of challenges for Treasury auctions in meeting their objectives. The inevitable rise in Treasury bond yields required to attract investors will further complicate the debt servicing obligations being incurred by the U.S. government.

The continuing erosion of the U.S. fiscal posture will inflict corresponding damage to the strength of the American dollar. The role of the U.S. dollar as the international reserve currency, and the ability of the Federal Reserve to print dollars at will, has provided the United States with the an ability to employ monetary policy as a backstop to the financial and economic crisis to a degree that cannot be matched by any other economy. However, embryonic discussions by policymakers and central bankers questioning the global status of the U.S. dollar will become increasingly concrete as the fiscal environment of the United States undergoes further deterioration in the period 2010-11. As the perception grows that the United States federal government is trapped in a fiscal trajectory that is unsustainable, the dollar will decline sharply in value. This descent will not be uniform, and at short intervals there will likely be temporary spikes in the value of the U.S. dollar. This will be precipitated by a "flight to safety" sentiment as other economies begin to falter in their economic recoveries, and by downturns in equities and commodities. However, in the long-term, the increasing belief by key decision-makers around the globe that the projected growth in America's national debt and annual debt servicing costs are not tenable will ultimately undermine the attributes that have maintained the strength of the dollar in spite of clear weaknesses in the American economy. As the U.S. dollar declines in value, it will further accelerate the deterioration of the fiscal imbalance in the public finances of the United States. In addition, it will inflict severe collateral damage on export-driven economies that depend directly or indirectly on the spending capacity of the

American consumer. A collapsing dollar will unleash major inflationary pressures on imported goods and commodities. The severe contraction in global trade that occurred in the immediate aftermath of the financial crisis will be replicated before the end of 2011.

In October 2000 the euro was valued at just over $0.82 U.S.; this figure peaked at a high of nearly $1.60 in July 2008. A "flight to safety" by investors improved the relative position of the dollar against the euro, however, by the summer of 2009, the euro had stabilized at over $1.44. This figure, significantly lower than the peak levels of 2008, still reflected a decline in the relative value of the U.S. dollar against the euro of more than 40% since 2000. Recent history and likely trends over the next 18-24 months point to the strong possibility of further double-digit declines in the relative value of the American dollar measured against major currencies in this timeframe. Such a precipitous decline in the dollar, should it in fact occur at levels we anticipate, will have a calamitous effect on the already fragile U.S. economy and financial system.

The continuing weaknesses in U.S. consumer spending, even with the technical ending of the recession, will exacerbate the balance sheet problems facing many American banks. Not only will an increasing number of near-prime and prime household mortgages go into default, adding to the already toxic subprime mortgages that nearly took down the global financial system; credit card debt and consumer loans will also become increasingly problematic. However, the most significant new danger that will confront banks in the United States and in other advanced economies will be the collapse of the commercial real estate market.

The deleveraging by American consumers and contracting disposable income driven by high unemployment rates will squeeze commercial property renters severely; retail developments, in particular large mall complexes, will become increasingly challenged in their ability to produce sufficient rental income to service their debt obligations. A rising tide of business bankruptcies will add further pressure on highly leveraged office and retail properties.

The subprime debacle in the housing market overwhelmingly impacted the largest U.S. banks and financial institutions. With commercial real estate, however, the pyramid becomes inverted. The bulk of the exposure to commercial real estate mortgages in the United States is held by financial institutions of small to medium size. Deutsche Bank real estate analyst Richard Parkus, testifying before a congressional committee in the summer of 2009, indicated that the four largest American banks have an average exposure of 2 percent of their balance sheets to commercial real estate. In contrast, the banking institutions that ranked between 30th and 100th in order of size had on average a 12 percent exposure to commercial real estate mortgages. What these figures suggest is that a massive collapse in the U.S. commercial real estate market will cripple a large number of regional and community banks, in comparison to a few "too big to fail" institutions stricken by the subprime housing disaster. When this occurs, round two of the banking crisis will be underway.

A large proportion of commercial real estate debt that was initiated when the valuations of commercial properties were at their peak will be coming due over the next 3 years, including $400 billion by the end of 2009, and nearly $2 trillion by 2012. With unemployment remaining at elevated levels, real disposable income shrinking and household savings rates at 5% or higher, it is our assessment that a significant proportion of these loans will become non-performing. In the prevailing economic climate, there

will exist no viable options in terms of refinancing and securitization. As with residential real estate, a glut of foreclosed commercial
properties will further depress prices, creating a vicious concentric
circle that will erode the balance sheets of a large number of
regional and mid-sized banks. We estimate that the impending
commercial real estate crash will create losses for U.S. banks of at
least $500 billion; in a worst case scenario this figure could reach as
high as $1.5 trillion.

In 2009 the number of bank failures rose precipitously, exceeding 80 financial institutions shut down by the FDIC by the end of
August 2009. In all of 2008, the year that the banking crisis exploded, 35 banks were shut down by the FDIC, and only 3 in 2007.
During the summer of 2009 the FDIC reported that the number of
problem banks and thrifts on its watch list had risen to 416 in Q2 of
2009. In the period 2010-11 we foresee a worsening of the banking
crisis, with potentially hundreds of banks and thrifts being closed
by the FDIC in this period. The FDIC will require massive recapitalization from the Treasury as its funds, based on premiums from
insured banks, will become depleted. Thus, the banking crisis,
even in the formative stage of its second phase, will exert negative
pressure on the overall fiscal situation for the federal government.

The deteriorating condition of America's banks will further exacerbate the squeeze on credit that will have stifled any tentative
recovery induced through massive sovereign deficits. Unemployment will remain high, further dampening a restoration of pre-
recessionary levels of consumer spending. Many economists will
perceive a re-entry into a recession, or the imminent risk of a
double dip economic contraction towards the latter part of 2010 or
early 2011. In this situation, the Obama administration is likely, if
reluctantly, to initiate a second round of heavy deficit-driven
economic stimulus spending. In large part these policy measures

will be dictated by political realities to a far greater extent than purely economic considerations. The mid-term congressional elections of 2010 and the upcoming presidential elections of 2012 will be crucial factors in raising the ceiling on the national debt in order to accommodate additional stimulus spending. Such an allocation may range between $200-500 billion dollars, depending on the unemployment rate and political polling data, and may possibly be structured in more than one stimulus package. The net result will be to further exacerbate the deteriorating fiscal posture of the United States federal government.

The weak employment market in the U.S. and further erosion of the balance sheets of America's banks will spark a rising tide of bank failures, as indicated above, and again jeopardize the largest financial institutions in America. The large banks we see as vulnerable to failure include those that have already been deemed as being "too big to fail" by the U.S. government, being the recipients of hundreds of billions of dollars of financial aid and guarantees from the taxpayers. These financial institutions include Citigroup and JP Morgan Chase. Furthermore, these banks, ranked among the top 5 in the United States in terms of assets, have a substantial exposure to derivatives, laying open the possibility of an AIG scenario involving global financial systemic risk in the event of an institutional meltdown. During the course of 2011, a banking crisis that will rival the collapse of Lehman Brothers in September of 2008 will confront decision makers in the United States with the unpalatable choice of either a taxpayer-funded bank bailout or accepting the liquidation of some banks that had previously been categorized as "too big to fail." The degree of financial support required to stabilize the American banking system will far exceed the initial investment made under the TARP program, which involved $700 billion.

In early 2009 the IMF estimated that the cost to the global financial system stemming from toxic assets was in the vicinity of $4 trillion, with three quarters of this figure derived from the collapse of the U.S. subprime mortgage market. NYU professor of economics Nouriel Roubini issued a similar analysis which placed a figure of $3.6 trillion in connection with the damage inflicted on the global financial system. In February 2009, U.S. Treasury Secretary Geithner estimated that $2 trillion might be required to salvage the nation's banking system.

It is our assessment that when round two of the banking crisis in the United States explodes with full fury, likely during the latter part of 2011 but possibly earlier, the degree of taxpayer support required for a systemic bailout will significantly exceed the estimates postulated in early 2009. This will be due to several factors; the accumulating damage resulting from an inability or unwillingness by the political echelon to comprehensively address the toxic assets as they existed after the collapse of Lehman Brothers; the additional destruction to balance sheet integrity due to new forms of asset erosion driven by emerging negative economic metrics; finally, the volatility of derivatives held by major banks that have a notional value far in excess of their assets.

While a definitive figure for a bailout of major financial institutions is difficult to postulate, it will almost certainly be tabulated in the trillions of dollars, as compared with the $700 billion TARP program approved by Congress in October 2008. We project that the cost of a bank bailout required by the scenario we foresee will likely be in the range of $3-5 trillion. This figure may possibly be even higher, if it is deemed essential to bailout the hundreds of small to mid-sized banks that will be vulnerable to collapse, but which fall below the threshold of "too big to fail." The cumulative damage that may result from hundreds of smaller banks being

liquidated might still render the U.S. banking system dysfunctional, even if the largest institutions are saved from collapse by
massive capital injections from the taxpayers.

The massive borrowing required to subsidize financial system
bailouts and additional economic stimulus packages will material-
ize at a point when the United States is already experiencing the
most precarious fiscal condition in its history. Policymakers will be
forced to initiate a massive increase in the national debt ceiling at a
time when the nation will have already been entrapped with
structural mega-deficits. This conjunction will prove unsustainable, leading to a catastrophic constriction in the flow of foreign
credit accessible to the U.S. Treasury. Simultaneously, bond yields
will rise to levels that will radically increase the cost of debt service
for the U.S., further exacerbating its fiscal conundrum. The United
States will be plunged into a far more severe economic and financial crisis.

When the revised national debt ceiling exceeds 100% of America's GDP, simultaneously with an annual deficit comprising at
least half of the annual budget of the federal government and
expanding contingent liabilities, a point will have been reached
whereby traditional economic policy measures, no matter how
liberally interpreted, will become inoperative. There are simply no
mathematical models that will allow the United States to sustain
the level of overseas borrowing and debt service payments it
would require to fully fund the bailout of its financial system and
continuation of economic stimulus measures.

In 2000, the total revenue of the U.S. federal government derived from taxes and other sources was $2.025 trillion, with expen-
ditures of $2.261 trillion and a gross national debt of $5.674 trillion.
For 2009 the Office of Management and Budget projected rever ¯
of $2.074 trillion, barely above the figure of nine years previc

an indication of the severity of the recession sparked by the collapse of the American housing market. For FY2009 government expenditures were projected at $3.563 trillion by OMB, an increase of 57% over the figure for 2000, while the national debt had exceeded $11.7 trillion, more than double the level of nine years prior to 2009. Factoring in stagnant or at best marginal GDP and government revenue growth, and a continuation of structural mega-deficits, it is a matter of certitude that the economic and financial costs of the next phase of the U.S. banking crisis we foresee will, in effect, "break the bank," plunging the United States into a profound fiscal cataclysm. This will precipitate the next phase of the global economic crisis, resulting in a severe worldwide depression.

7

2012-2015:
Synchronized Global Depression

The sovereign debt crisis in the United States, which we anticipate to have been unleashed by 2012 due to the factors previously outlined, will plunge the global economy into a severe free fall contraction. Accelerating the decline of global macroeconomic indicators will be the replication of America's fiscal crisis in many other nation states, including advanced and developing economies.

Among the other advanced economies that are at high risk of a paralyzing fiscal crisis is the United Kingdom. As with the United States, the UK absorbed a massive degree of public debt in order to bailout its banking system. Also in parallel with the United States, a significant decline in residential real estate valuations and the capacity of consumers to incur new debt has degraded government revenue while simultaneously increasing outlays for stimulus spending and social costs related to high rates of unemployment; in 2009 the annual UK fiscal deficit was £175 billion.

These factors have driven the UK's annual deficit to GDP ratio to a level above 10% for the foreseeable future. The impact on the overall public debt of the United Kingdom has been severe. In the three year period between 2007 and 2010 the nation's total public

debt as a ratio to GDP increased from 38% to 67%. It is our view
that the present fiscal trajectory of the UK will grow the debt to
GDP ratio to a level approaching 100% by 2012, and will likely
exceed that figure by 2015, if not earlier.

A continuing weak economy, stagnant growth at best and vulnerable asset values prior to 2012 will place further pressure on the
balance sheets of UK banks, requiring additional taxpayer bailouts,
as will be the case with the United States. This will place the
United Kingdom in a dangerous fiscal position, as it will experience insoluble challenges in its efforts to borrow through auctions of Treasury gilts the overseas credit it will require. It is our
projection that the United Kingdom will share with the U.S. the
high probability of entering a profound sovereign debt crisis
around 2012. The looming fiscal predicament facing the United
Kingdom will be complicated by a likely political transition, with
the Conservative Party taking control of Parliament.

Though key decision makers within the UK political establishment are aware of the unsustainability of the nation's structural
mega-deficits, they will have run out of options by 2012. Cutting
spending and/or raising taxes at a time when the UK will still be
experiencing sluggish economic growth at best and high unemployment will inevitably unleash a renewed recession. That, in
turn, will create new deficits, defeating the intended objective of
tax increases and public spending reductions. Conversely, maintaining structural mega-deficits will lead to a fiscal calamity. The
trap that the UK will find itself in, as with the United States, is that
once an advanced economy's gross public debt to GDP ratio
reaches 100%, the component of the national budget devoted to
debt service accumulates at a rate that is beyond the ability of a
sovereign with low growth rates, at best, and a demographically
aging population, to reign in.

The Eurozone, which will have experienced modestly improved economic metrics during 2010-2011, will incur devastating afflictions to its banking and financial system by 2012, due primarily to the collapse of national economies throughout Eastern Europe. Much of the exposure involves mortgages on residential and commercial real estate in Eastern Europe that were underwritten in euros. A consequence of the global economic crisis has been the collapse in value of many Eastern European currencies in relation to the euro, leading to a wave of defaults. In particular, the Baltic states, Ukraine and Hungary will be especially vulnerable to mortgage meltdowns, in the process inflicting debilitating blows on the integrity of bank balance sheets throughout Western Europe, particularly in Austria and Italy.

The looming danger of a catastrophic financial and fiscal crisis impacting the Eurozone was anticipated in February 2009, when a confidential document was leaked to the British newspaper, The Daily Telegraph, from a source within the European Commission, which projected an apocalyptic level of danger to the Eurozone's financial system. The European Commission serves as the executive branch that rules over the 27 nations that constitute the European Union, and is based in Brussels. In the confidential EC document disclosed by The Daily Telegraph, its authors concluded that European banks may be holding as much as 18.6 trillion euros in toxic assets, roughly equivalent to $24 trillion. The secret document issued a stark warning to the political leaders of the member states of the EU that the amount of money required to salvage the European banking system, which had only months before received its own version of a TARP-style bailout, would defy the financial and political capacity of the countries that comprise the European Union. The language in the EC document stated the cold facts with harsh simplicity: "estimates of total expected asset write-downs suggest that the budgetary costs-actual and contingent-of asset relief could be very large both in absolute terms and relative to GDP in member states." This assessment recognized that whatever portion of the $24 trillion of toxic assets European banks have on their balance sheets that will need to be written off, the ultimate figure would clearly be substantial, and could not be financed by the European Union. To put that $24 trillion worst-case figure in perspective, it exceeds by at least six trillion dollars the combined GDP of the entire EU, and dwarfs the GDP figure for the United States, which stood at $14 trillion in 2009.

The precipitating event for the Great Depression of the 1930s was the stock market crash on Wall Street in 1929. However, the trigger than transformed an American financial crisis into a worldwide economic depression was the collapse of a major Austrian bank, the Credit-Anstalt, in 1931. The global financial architecture of our contemporary world has a vastly higher degree of interconnection and synchronicity than existed during the 1930s. This would suggest that a major banking failure in Western or Central Europe would inflict massive collateral damage on the global financial system.

Given all the above factors, we project that by 2012 the Euro-zone, along with the UK, will be mired in deep recession and overwhelmed by systemic failure of major financial institutions. The fiscal limitations of sovereigns, forecasted by the European Commission in 2009, will render them incapable of initiating taxpayer bailouts of their banks and major corporations that are confronted with insolvency.

Japan, while technically remaining the world's second largest economy, will be facing a renewed recession and severe fiscal challenges in 2012, rendering its national economy vulnerable to the downturn that will have stricken its major export markets. A change in government in 2009 placed new elites in power, with promises to constituents that have committed the government to spending priorities that exceed the nation's fiscal capacity.

In 2008 Japan's public debt to GDP ratio approached 200%, a much higher level than in the United States. Factors that have mitigated the large deficits and national debt level in the past have been the high savings rate of the population, allowing Tokyo to grow its debt load through primarily domestic sources of credit. However, collapsing export markets and the looming demographic challenges facing Japan, in particular an aging population and declining birthrate, will pose far more severe challenges to the stability of the nation's finances. It is our view that by 2012 the Japanese political echelon will be compelled to restrain public spending, which in turn will dampen domestic consumption simultaneously with the sharp drop in export earnings that we anticipate. This will unleash a severe economic contraction, internally, while externally negating Japan as a significant purchaser of U.S. Treasuries.

In 2009 Japan ranked as the second largest holder of U.S. debt, its $700 billion holding of Treasury debt instruments exceeded only by China. If Tokyo ceases to be a substantial source of overseas credit at a time when we believe the U.S. government will be facing staggering bailout costs for the next phase in the American banking crisis, there are unlikely to be alternative sovereign wealth funds that can compensate. This virtually ensures that by 2012 the United States will be faced with a chronic fiscal crisis of staggering proportions.

The impending budgetary crisis that will confront the U.S. will occur in a timeframe when all sectors of the United States economy will be suffocating under the weight of an unprecedented degree of leverage. In 1933, at the height of the Great Depression, total credit market debt in the United States, inclusive of government, households, the corporate and financial sectors represented 260% of GDP. In the early 1980s, it stood at about 170% of GDP. However, in Q1 of 2009 the total U.S. credit market debt to GDP ratio had soared to an historically high level of 373%.

Though there will likely be modest initial deleveraging by American households prior to 2012, this will be massively offset by mounting public indebtedness. Furthermore, a high rate of unemployment will spark an overall rise in household and corporate leveraging towards the latter part of 2011. Further massive government borrowing to fund future financial system bailouts and economic stimulus measures, in conjunction with continuing structural mega-deficits, points to a total debt to GDP ratio exceeding 450%, a level far higher than during the most severe period of the Great Depression.

It is our assessment that it will not be possible for the United States government to borrow sufficient capital from overseas creditors to fund its financial obligations and commitments. This will be exacerbated by the highly leveraged position of the American household sector, negating domestic investors as a significant market for expanded Treasury auctions. All these factors combined will, in effect, render the government of the United States as being in a condition of virtual insolvency.

Simultaneously with the unhinging of America's fiscal posture, an even more dangerous off-balance sheet reality will become a highly relevant factor in the period after 2012; the underfunding of the U.S. Social Security and Medicare system. As the U.S. budget deficit has soared since 1980, ironically the Social Security system has been in surplus; the U.S. Treasury has, in effect, borrowed money from the Social Security trust fund to cover revenue shortfalls incurred by the federal government. Decision makers within the U.S. political establishment frequently subtract the IOUs created by Treasury in exchange for Social Security surplus dollars from the gross national debt, as though this is an obligation that can be defaulted on without consequence (the net balance derived from subtraction of federal liabilities for retirees from the national debt is defined as the public debt by U.S. decision makers). Yet, many observers are keenly aware that the Social Security and Medicare system will eventually be in deficit, and at an accelerating rate, based on demographic trends and future economic growth rates, correlated with government obligations made to future retirees.

Even before the onset of the global financial crisis in 2008, an authoritative assessment was made regarding the stark underfunding of the Medicare and Social Security infrastructure in the United States. David M. Walker, who served as the Comptroller-General of the United States from 1998 to 2008, issued a warning prior to the onset of the global financial and economic crisis that America faced more than $50 trillion in unfunded obligations due to Medicare and Social Security. Walker's warnings were ignored; rather than allocating revenue to ensure these future liabilities were fully funded, or restructure future retirement entitlements to conform with fiscal reality, Congress and the federal government simply deferred addressing the pending Social Security and Medicare funding crisis.

The global economic crisis and its impact on long-term growth prospects for the U.S. economy have, in our view, made the pending Medicare and Social Security funding crisis both more substantial and imminent than originally framed by David Walker. Richard W. Fisher, President of the Dallas Federal Reserve, delivered a speech to the Commonwealth Club of California back in May 2008, in which he indicated that the authentic national debt of the United States, using generally accepted accounting principals, was nearly $100 trillion, or nine times the official national debt as of the fall of 2009. Putting this surreal as well as apocalyptic number in perspective, Fisher said, "With a total population of 304 million, from infants to the elderly, the per-person payment to the federal treasury would come to $330,000. This comes to $1.3 million per family of four, over 25 times the average household's income."

The collision that will have occurred by 2012 involving the truncated revenue capacity of the U.S. taxpayers, staggering bailout costs for new systemic financial crises, and explosive growth in the national debt and yearly deficits will render the treatment of gross underfunding of entitlements for America's aging population as an off-balance sheet calculation no longer tenable. Foreign creditors and the bond market will be compelled by turbulent circumstances to view the credit worthiness and long-term fiscal capacity of the United States with an unprecedented degree of critical objectivity.

In 2009, amid the rhetoric emanating from policymakers that the vast sovereign deficits required to pay for bailing out the financial system were a short-term expedient measure, and that an exit strategy would lead to a new era of fiscal nirvana, several leading actors within the bond market were already voicing scepticism. Once such voice was the Co-Chief Investment Officer at Pacific Investment Management Company, otherwise known as Pimco, Bill Gross. Pimco is the largest bond dealer in the world, making it an essential institution for the marketing of sovereign debt. Gross stated at that time, "While policymakers, including the President and Treasury Secretary Geithner, assure voters and financial markets alike that such a path is unsustainable and that a return to fiscal conservatism is just around the recovery's corner, it is hard to comprehend exactly how that more balanced rabbit can be pulled out of Washington's hat."

By 2012 it will be clear that the U.S. government has no magical hat to pull a rabbit out of. It will then be facing the dire circumstance of national insolvency. When it is fully revealed that the United States has been plunged into a catastrophic fiscal crisis, a number of existentially foreboding financial and economic repercussions will immediately unfold. These will include:

- Demise of the U.S. dollar as the international reserve currency. The loss of its privileged status will undermine the value of the American dollar, and its reputation as a safe haven. Investors and sovereign funds will flee the dollar at high velocity
- Collapse in value of the U.S. dollar, based on the above factors
- Collapse in price of Treasury bills, coinciding with downgrading of U.S. government debt. The loss of AAA status will be followed by a market view of Treasuries as being synonymous with junk bonds, concomitant with a substantial rise in Treasury bond yields essential for attracting even a reduced level of buyers

The above developments will precipitate a wave of bank closures that will sweep America, with an insolvent federal government unable to intervene with bailouts and backstops. The FDIC will run out of funding, negating its capacity to honor its guarantees to the nation's depositors. This will unleash a run on the nation's banks, a loss of public confidence in the U.S. banking system, and the virtual collapse of a significant component of the American credit market.

Coinciding with the collapse of much of America's banking sector will be the radical curtailment of U.S. government operations due to acute funding shortfalls, with similar phenomena unfolding with respect to state, county and municipal governing authorities throughout the United States. In the immediate wake of the onset of the U.S. fiscal crisis, we foresee an attempt by the federal government to utilize IOUs in lieu of cash disbursements, replicating the experience of California during that state's fiscal crisis in 2009. The insolvency of governmental authorities throughout the United States, combined with the implosion of the American banking and financial system, will force a large proportion of businesses, including those large, medium and small, in all economic sectors, into liquidation. Enterprises that survive will be required to reduce payrolls drastically. The above factors will lead to unemployment rates that will rise to levels not witnessed in the United States since the Great Depression of the 1930s.

The fiscal collapse of the U.S. federal government by 2012, replicated by other American governmental authorities, and the repercussions to the general economy that will ensue, will create a radical economic contraction through 2015. Using 2007 as a base year, just prior to the onset of the recession triggered by the subprime meltdown, we estimate that U.S. GDP will have contracted in excess of 10% by 2015. The rate of economic contraction and its duration between 2007 and 2015 which we project will meet the technical definition of a depression.

The economic devastation that is likely to occur in the United States in the period 2012-2015 will be unprecedented. In effect, at least temporarily, the U.S. will be in the throes of an economic and financial collapse. In such a scenario, there is an extended period of economic paralysis. Commercial activity grinds to a halt due to credit evaporation and elevated counterparty risk aversion. Public and private sectors are transformed into shadows of their former existence, operating on primitive lines such as barter arrangements in lieu of banking systems and sophisticated financial and credit markets. While historically an economic collapse is seldom a permanent condition, depending on policy responses its duration and severity can be long-lasting.

Beyond the impact of a national economic collapse on the individual nation state is the collateral effect on the global economy. In the past the world has witnessed the collapse of national economies, such as Argentina in the early 1990s and Iceland in 2008, without seismic global impact. However, these two examples involved nation states that comprised a relatively small component of global GDP. Iceland, for example, with a population of only 300,000 had a GDP in 2008 of $12.6 billion, representing a mere 2/100th of one percent of global GDP.

The economic collapse of the largest economy in the world would have vastly more disastrous consequences for the global economy. With a GDP in 2009 of $14 trillion, the United States represents more than 20% of the global GDP of $60 trillion. As both the largest consumer and debtor nation in the world, its economic demise due primarily to a catastrophic fiscal crisis would ensure that a synchronized global depression would be unleashed. This impending worldwide economic contraction would be further facilitated by multiple national financial crises outlined previously in this report.

As with the case of a collapsing star resulting from an exploding supernova, the aggregate size of an imploding economy determines its destructive impact on the economic universe. In the realm of physics an imploding star that exceeds three solar masses undergoes a total collapse until it is transformed into a black hole. We believe that similar mathematical laws apply to economic

phenomena involving nation states operating within the framework of a global economic and financial system. The weight of
America's debt obligations, their global interconnection and
widespread leverage regarding both public and private sectors, in
conjunction with her massive share of total global consumption
derived from imported goods and commodities, in effect becomes
the economic equivalent of three solar masses. The collapse of the
U.S. economy, without question, will devastate every other national economy on the planet. Should that collapse be total, the
world economy risks witnessing the United States being transformed from the global engine of growth into an economic equivalent of a black hole, with its potential for universal credit defaults
on a massive scale becoming an event horizon that will suck the
essence out of the global economy with the mass and energy of a
total gravitational collapse.

As with the United States, we envision that global GDP will have
contracted by at least 10% by 2015, as compared with 2007. Virtually
every metric of global economic performance, including trade and
credit flows, will be severely attenuated in the timeframe 2012-2015.
Historically high rates of unemployment will become a universal
reality, with grave social implications for virtually every country.

In past recessions that created high rates of joblessness in national economies, migration was often the safety valve that enabled
the unemployed in one nation to relocate to other economies less
affected by recessionary forces. In a synchronized global depression, however, there will be no refuge from high unemployment, at
least through 2015 and likely years afterward. With every nation
state coping with dysfunctional economies, unemployed popula-
tions without a migration option will facilitate social unrest and
destabilizing forces. These will occur in every country, however,
the United States will be especially vulnerable.

The realization that the vast levels of public indebtedness brought on by the political establishment, based on the claim that this was the price for renewed economic growth, have not proven efficacious, will likely lead to widespread alienation by the American people towards their leaders. A collective feeling of betrayal directed at the U.S. elites will probably become widespread among the middle class and working poor in the United States, exacerbating already existing political fault lines. The U.S. presidential election of 2012 will coincide, in our view, with the onset of the fiscal crisis we project. The feeling of helplessness that will pervade a large segment of the U.S. population leaves open the possibility that demagogic forces may arise within the U.S. political culture, creating a whole new vortex stemming from the economic crisis, with unforeseen global consequences.

Irrespective of the outcome of the 2012 U.S. presidential election, we do not foresee new policy measures and fiscal initiatives that would mitigate the severe economic contraction and government fiscal crisis that will occur through 2015. In our view, neither political party is likely to advocate significant tax increases or deep spending cuts. In particular, both major political parties will remain committed to vast expenditures on the military and national security activities, and maintaining social entitlements, especially to retirees, that cannot be sustained by America's fiscal capacity. Though some policy differences do exists between the major political parties in the United States, we do not assess these as being significant enough to alter the outcome of the fiscal crisis that we expect to occur by 2012.

The challenge that will confront the next presidential administration in the United States post-2012 will be the collision between global economic and financial reality and domestic political dogma and ideology. Volatile bond markets, the downgrading of U.S.

government debt within the sovereign debt markets and stagnant or contracting government revenues will impose harsh economies upon the United States, regardless of Washington's ideological commitments. Ultimately, in the face of government insolvency, the political establishment in Washington will be compelled to conform to the painful realities of a global economic depression, in which the United States is the insolvent epicentre.

China will be severely impacted by a global economic depression stemming from a crippling fiscal crisis in the United States. It stands to incur substantial losses in value to its investments and sovereign wealth assets denominated in U.S. dollars. The contraction in global trade will severely undercut export earnings. Furthermore, the vast stimulus spending program initiated by Beijing in 2009 has created the danger of asset bubbles in domestic real estate and equity markets, which may explode with deflationary force by 2012. All these factors create critical challenges for China's leadership.

In spite of China's vulnerability to the next phase of the global economic crisis, there exist unique strengths with respect to that nation's economy that provide her with the potential to endure the severe worldwide economic contraction we anticipate for 2012-2015 far better than any other major economy. Beijing's accumulated trade surplus has provided her with sovereign wealth resources that can create options not available to her economic competitors. How effective those resources are will be, in large part, determined by steps undertaken by the central government to limit the damage to those assets due to the plummeting value of the U.S. dollar.

Chinese authorities are aware that a rapid sell-off of its U.S. dollar holdings will signal the market in a manner that will facilitate a rapid depreciation in the greenback's value relative to other currencies. The challenge that Chinese authorities must face is the correct calibration of implementing policies such as limiting purchases of U.S. Treasuries while simultaneously deploying U.S. dollar holdings for acquisition of strategic economic assets, including overseas mining concessions and oil leases.

How well China navigates the emerging U.S. dollar collapse will determine its ability to cope with the likely social upheavals that will confront her amid a synchronized global depression. High unemployment and growing ethnic tension represent the most serious domestic repercussions that will result from the downturn in the domestic economy stemming from a massive global economic contraction. A strong central government, with significant technocratic skills organic to its composition, provides China with advantages, in terms of flexibility and timing, with respect to enacting policy responses appropriate to the evolving phases of the economic crisis.

Forecasting the impact on China's GDP in the period 2012-2015 is complicated by the lack of transparency with regard to official economic statistics and the characteristics of Beijing's hybrid economic model, incorporating elements of central planning and free enterprise capitalism. During the onset of the global economic crisis following the collapse of Lehman Brothers, China maintained high GDP growth figures despite the overall contraction of the global economy. However, those growth figures were almost entirely driven by government stimulus spending, a policy response that will be difficult to replicate in the more severe crisis we foresee after 2012. In real terms, we believe there will be a contraction of the Chinese economy between 2012-2015, with the possibility of stagnation as opposed to negative growth by the end of that period. Due to the unique advantages available to policymakers in Beijing, we anticipate that the overall contraction of the Chinese economy in the timeframe 2012-2015 will be in the range of 3-5% in real terms, significantly less severe than the overall global economy, though official statistics may proclaim a more optimistic measurement. While the contraction we project will reflect stronger economic performance compared with other major advanced and developing economies, it still will represent a significant reduction in China's economic performance measured against its peak capacity, and will likely lead to a substantial rise in unemployment.

In a major economic downturn, including severe recessions and depressions, deflation is the major tendency in terms of abnormal price equilibrium. However, central banks in many economies, in particular the United States and United Kingdom, have engaged in substantial and extended quantitative easing as the primary monetary response to the global economic crisis. Furthermore, monetary policy has been utilized as a mechanism for financing sovereign deficits through monetization of the debt. These measures are inherently inflationary. The contradiction between asset deflation and monetary policies that are inflationary will lead to the period of 2012-2015 being characterized by asymmetrical price volatility, or APV. The emergence of APV as a significant economic factor during the onset of the synchronized global depression we are forecasting will complicate policy responses by sovereigns and protective strategies by investors and private corporate entities.

An early indicator of the destructive capacity of APV during times of financial and economic turmoil was the unprecedented price explosion and collapse with respect to oil exports during the summer and fall of 2008. As noted previously in this report, the rapid escalation of oil commodity prices in 2008 magnified the global economic repercussions stemming from the collapse of the subprime mortgage market in the United States. The subsequent retreat in oil prices inflicted economic damage on petroleum exporting countries and undermined the efficacy of price hedging strategies.

The global economic depression beginning in 2012 will incorporate aspects that will render many advanced and emerging economies as being especially vulnerable to APV forces. A major contributor to this scenario will be the collapse of the U.S. dollar resulting from America's fiscal crisis and the loss of the dollar's status as the international reserve currency. This may lead to a situation where commodity and asset prices fall in real terms due to shrinking demand, while the nominal price actually increases due to market-driven currency devaluation. Asymmetrical price volatility will create a sense of global urgency on the question of defining a new international reserve currency.

Even with global economic contraction, carbon based energy commodities, including crude oil and natural gas, may experience a rise in price towards 2015, due to the growing perception that peak oil production has been realized. While this prospect has been forecasted and speculated on for more than a decade, a growing consensus on this issue will have been reached by the onset of the global economic depression. Any perceived signs of an economic recovery, or even a moderation in the projected free fall in consumer demand and industrial production, will likely create strong upward price pressure on oil exports. While China will be somewhat immunized from the full effects of future oil price inflation due to her strategic acquisition of external sources of petroleum supplies, her major economic competitors will face severe challenges.

The United States, as the largest net importer of carbon based energy supplies, is the most vulnerable national economy to the ramifications of peak oil. The collapse of the dollar will lead to oil exporters pricing their product in other currencies, creating immense difficulties in financing a high rate of oil importation. Ultimately, the lack of financial resources will compel the U.S. to severely curtail her oil imports, which in turn will lead to further economic dislocation. With no alternative sources of energy available in the near term to compensate for the displacement of a previously high rate of oil importation, the implications for the American economy during the period 2012-2015 will be severe, further exacerbating an already pre-existing high rate of domestic economic contraction.

A final dimension of the next phase of the global economic crisis will be the impact of financial derivatives. The vast sums of money poured into AIG in the fall of 2008 and subsequently to contain the damage from this firm's credit default swaps are both a warning and a harbinger of the dangers that lie before the world's interconnected financial system. The price tag for U.S. taxpayers of just one firm's CDS business was initially $180 billion. However, if there are a string of bank failures involving the United States, UK and Eurozone, in particular the "too big to fail" institutions, the potential losses may be incalculable. This is in large part due to the lack of transparency concerning derivative financial products, especially credit default and interest rate swaps. To a large extent, these unregulated products of exotic financial engineering exist below the radar, amidst the opaqueness of a vast global shadow banking system. Estimates regarding the notional values of derivatives vary widely, raging from $500 trillion to an inconceivable $1.2 quadrillion. However, assuming the actual number lies within the range of these figures, it represents many multiplies of global GDP.

In a worst case scenario, the financial collapse of several of the world's leading commercial and investment banks, each with a significant exposure to derivatives, within a confined period of time, may spark a chain reaction in which financial derivatives become fissionable contracts that self-destruct. This would ultimately lead to the complete meltdown of the global financial system, and utter collapse of the world economy.

In 1873, the Vienna stock exchange crashed, sparking what was once called the Great Depression, but has since the depression of the 1930s been labelled by historians as the Long Depression. For decades, the world's major economies were wracked by a series of depressions, near depressions and severe recessions, with interludes of brief though deceptive recoveries. The United States did not emerge from the enduring and destructive impact of the Long Depression until after 1901.

It is our view that the economic contraction that began in 1873, as opposed to 1929, is more analogous to the threat that hangs over our contemporary globalized economy like the sword of Damocles. In the event that financial derivatives act as the incendiary fuel that accelerates all the other negative factors leading to an economic depression by 2012, the period of global economic purgatory that will be endured before the emergence of a sustained recovery may be measured not in years, but in decades.

8

Conclusions and Recommendations

This report projects that a global depression will occur during the period 2012-2015, propelled by a sovereign debt crisis enabled by massive bailouts and public stimulus packages that began after the collapse of Lehman Brothers in September 2008. A principle finding in our analysis is that the United States national debt will exceed 100% of GDP by 2012, and that the combination of growing debt service payments, public and corporate entitlements and looming systemic failures in America's financial system requiring unprecedented government bailouts, will impose an unsustainable fiscal burden on the federal government, leading to its financial collapse and insolvency.

Many economists who are aware of the dramatic growth in the national debt of the U.S. have nevertheless argued that this expansion of public indebtedness is justified. They maintain that government deficits during the global economic crisis will prevent a more severe contraction of the national economy, and eventually restore GDP growth. That future growth, maintain the supporters of structural mega-deficits, will assure the eventual receding of the national debt to GDP ratio. One economist who has adopted this posture is Paul Krugman, winner of the 2008 Nobel Prize for economics. A major argument advanced by Krugman is that massive government debts incurred during World War II grew the national debt to a level above 100% of GDP, however that ratio contracted substantially within a few years. Krugman has also claimed that massive public indebtedness and deficits do not impose inflationary pressures during a severe economic crisis.

We believe that the comparison made by several economists, including Paul Krugman, between the current economic environment confronting the United States and the post-World War II economy is spurious and invalid. The United States ended World War II with a labor force, including a substantial military, which was fully employed but had been restricted in the opportunities to spend disposable income. This was due to rationing on basic commodities such as foodstuffs, and the termination of production of major consumer durables such as automobiles owing to industrial mobilization in support of the war effort. After VJ day the pent-up consumer demand exploded, while consumer goods remained in short supply in the immediate post-war period. The result was a combination of real growth and high inflation, both dynamics contributing to the attenuation of the national debt to GDP ratio. Furthermore, the federal government was able to drastically reduce military spending, eliminating structural megadeficits, thus limiting the growth of the national debt in nominal terms. Sharply rising consumer demand was able to generate massive private sector expansion, thus compensating for the contraction of military expenditures.

In 1946, the U.S. national debt to GDP ratio reached its highest level, 121%. By 1948, that ratio had declined significantly, at 93.7%. Now, let us observe the inflation rate during this period: 8.3% in 1946, a staggering 14.4% in 1947 and 8.1% in 1948. These figures clearly demonstrate that having a level of gross national debt exceeding 100% of the GDP does have inflationary consequences, and suggests that inflation in turn reduces the real value of the nominal public debt as a proportion of national GDP. The other factor that reduced the debt to GDP level in the immediate postwar period was the massive expansion of the domestic economy. Furthermore, and often ignored by economists who attempt to use World War II economics as a rationalization for massive public debts, the source of funding for Washington's deficit was dramatically different from the current situation. For the reasons indicated above, wage earners accumulated capital, but had limited recourse for spending it. The U.S. government therefore had a domestic source of credit available to it at relatively low interest rates, largely based on the sale of war bonds to the general public.

Contemporary America lacks the domestic manufacturing and engineering base that existed in 1945. The United States has been transformed into an economy far removed from the "arsenal of democracy" that existed in World War II. While highly dependent on foreign imports that encompass both raw commodities and finished industrial and consumer goods, the U.S. has replaced manufacturing capacity with the massive growth of the financial sector. The events that began with the collapse of the subprime mortgage market and led to the extinction of Lehman Brothers comprise only the first stage of a tectonic economic shift. When the next stage of the banking crisis erupts, we assert, based on the data and observations contained in this report, that the United States, both in terms of the federal government and overall national economy, will lack the fiscal capacity to avoid calamity.

In the dire circumstances that will confront governmental authorities post-2012, there are likely to be a host of hastily improvised and ad hoc policy measures adopted by the U.S. and other major economies engulfed by the projected sovereign debt crisis.

Ultimately, insolvent governments, the United States in particular, will be faced with three policy options:

- Increase public taxation while dramatically cutting spending
- Reduce the real value of the national debt through the hidden taxation of inflation
- Default on the national debt

These are all existentially foreboding policy options, and politicians will be tempted to delay formulating a strategic decision that will impose severe pain on their constituencies for as long as possible. However, market and financial realities will ensure that delay only compounds the public costs of the global economic crisis. In weighing these policy options, there are no good choices, only a cost benefit analysis of what direction imposes the least pain on society, and offers the most rapid exit from economic depression to a sustained path towards recovery.

The monetary policies that the U.S. Federal Reserve has maintained since the onset of the global economic crisis, in particular quantitative easing and a zero interest rate policy, or ZIRP, point to a strategy of inflating down the value of the national debt, though policymakers will undoubtedly publicly claim otherwise. This is a platform of short-term expediency, for it enables sovereigns to exact a hidden tax on its citizens. As the crisis evolved and many governments began assuming staggering levels of public debt, a number of prominent economists have advocated a targeted inflation rate in the range of 6% as the most efficacious policy response for reducing the national debt to GDP correlation.

It is our recommendation that sovereigns do not employ inflation as a deliberative policy response for coping with their national debt. In particular, this attempt at programmed inflation will inevitably prove catastrophic for those countries most in jeopardy from unsustainable debt to GDP ratios, including the United States and the UK. The historical experience with planned inflation implemented by central banks is that it is virtually impossible to control once the inflationary genie is released from its bottle, and the long-term social destabilization that ensues can lead to unintended, calamitous geopolitical consequences. The most notable example of inflation as monetary policy run amok was the experience of Weimar Germany, which depreciated its own currency in order to cope with the financial burden imposed on her as a result of war reparations stemming from that nation's defeat in the First World War. The outcome was a hyperinflationary spiral; in late 1923 the exchange rate for a single United States dollar was 4,200,000,000,000 German marks.

A component of engineered inflation is the purchase of a sovereign's Treasury bonds by the national entity's central bank. This policy response is otherwise known as monetization of the debt. In effect, a central bank merely prints money, loans the conjured capital to the sovereign, to compensate for its failure to cover its budgetary deficits through conventional bond auctions. Such a procedure, implemented with abandon, will inevitably destroy the fundamental value and credibility of a national currency. Furthermore, while debt monetization may in theory appear as an effective means of creating liquidity for an insolvent sovereign, the extreme risk of severe hyperinflation that is a corollary to such a reckless monetary policy will ensure that tax revenue remains insufficient to cover a budget deficit that is perpetually growing in nominal terms.

Defaulting on the national debt is another approach that has at various times been enacted by sovereigns. In many cases, national defaults are employed as negotiating strategies by sovereigns, in an effort to formulate an agreement with the nation's creditors to restructure debt payments so that their impact on the national budget does not impose unsustainable economic and social costs. In a scenario involving Third World countries, it is often the IMF that intervenes, leading to an agreement involving bridge financing to the sovereign conditional on the acceptance of fiscal and monetary reforms and the imposition of budgetary constraints.

In our view, defaulting on the national debt would be a strategic error by policymakers in major economies, especially in the United States. In a best case scenario, it would bring only a very brief interlude of fiscal relief, followed by a hurricane of long-term catastrophic consequences. The credit worthiness of the U.S. would be permanently destroyed; major creditors, including China and Japan, would suffer massive financial losses, facilitating their transformation into hostile economic adversaries that would deny any future credit to the United States. This would perpetuate the fiscal insolvency of the U.S. and irreparably destroy her status as a major economic actor. Furthermore, defaulting on debt is not a one-way street. Foreign governments and corporations with outstanding debts to American financial institutions would feel no restraint in replicating the debt default option, if this course were to be pursued by the U.S. government.

Unfortunately, in the aftermath of the synchronized global depression we envision as beginning in 2012, political actors in the United States may be persuaded to proclaim debt default as a nationalistic solution to America's monumental economic problems. In the context of America's current political culture, particularly in regard to a low level of comprehension of general economics by the majority of the population, it is not inconceivable that such a fatally flawed approach can be marketed to the electorate as a populist cure to the suffocating reality of the national debt. If debt default ever became the policy response of the U.S. government towards its acute fiscal crisis, we forecast with high confidence the total collapse of the American economy, with a parallel disintegration of social cohesion.

It is our view that the only prescription for the fiscal crisis that will drive the projected synchronized global depression is a carefully formulated and calibrated series of draconian spending cuts and tax increases by sovereigns confronted with structural mega-deficits and excessive national debt to GDP ratios. This recommendation applies especially to policymakers in the United States, despite the formidable political opposition to adopting such policy measures.

The most important component of spending by the U.S. federal government that should be targeted for drastic downsizing is its bloated national security budget. Though the official Defence Department budget is in the range of $600 billion per year, a figure that exceeds the next 25 largest military budgets combined, this is only a partial indication of the corrosive impact the American military industrial complex has had on the deterioration of the nation's fiscal posture. For example, most of the spending on nuclear weapons allocated by the U.S. Congress is not found within the Pentagon budget, but is actually appropriated through the Department of Energy. Many other funding areas, including medical care for veterans, and especially intelligence activities conducted by a myriad of agencies, including the Central Intelligence Agency and National Security Agency, must be added to the Defence Department budget in order to aggregate the actual military and national security spending by the United States. Our estimate is that this figure approaches $1 trillion annually, or nearly a third of the entire annual budget of the federal government of the United States.

We believe that the United States, in the midst of an acute fiscal and economic crisis, cannot justify a level of military and security expenditures required for the maintenance of a global empire. In our view, total U.S. expenditures within the national security arena should be reduced by 70%, falling into a range of $300 billion per year. While this drastic contraction in fiscal support for the military industrial complex will sharply reduce the capability of the United States to project military power globally, it is our view that this allocation, when combined with wise strategic, doctrinal and diplomatic choices, will be adequate for the defence of the nation within the current security environment. An important aspect of this policy recommendation involves the termination of the U.S. military presence in Iraq, and the resolution of the most immediate security threats to the U.S. that might emerge from Afghanistan, in a manner that removes the requirement for a permanent expeditionary force being maintained in that country.

In addition to a massive reduction in spending on national security activities, the U.S. Congress must eliminate all subsidies to corporations and businesses, as well as dispensable contracts with private consultants and contractors. In effect, the federal government must impose a fiscal diet on itself, restricting spending only to those activities that are essential for the national interest.

The looming insolvency of the Social Security and Medicare system must be dealt with on an urgent and permanent basis, as opposed to being perpetually placed on the backburner. All the other recommendations in this report will be rendered mute unless the whole question of funding retirement benefits and medical care in the United States is resolved on a permanent basis. We believe that this area's resolution requires a coordinated approach involving a limited reduction in benefits, a delay in eligibility based on actuarial data on extended life spans, in conjunction with a new approach towards funding Social Security and Medicare.

At present, the funding of Social Security in particular has been conceptually flawed. Though in theory the U.S. has a progressive tax system, along with other advanced economies, in reality it approaches a flat tax system that favors the wealthiest citizens at the expense of the middle class. This is due to the separation of retirement taxes from income tax revenue, and the manner in which they are generated. At present, on top of federal income tax, a separate FICA tax is paid to finance the Social Security system. In 2009 the Social Security tax was set at a flat rate of 6.2% for employed wage earners, up to a maximum income of $106,800 with no FICA tax on income above that ceiling.

We recommend to policymakers that the present separate tax system for funding Social Security be scrapped, along with the notion of a Social Security trust fund. In substitution, a new federal income tax table should be constructed, with progressive rates that would shift the burden of funding retiree benefits and medical care from the American middle class to the most affluent income earners. Retirement benefits would be established as annual budgetary allocations, with benefits matched to fiscal realities, and structured so as not to consume a disproportionate component of annual tax revenue. This approach would eliminate the menacing danger of unfunded liabilities for Social Security and Medicare, and contribute substantially to reconstructing the credit worthiness of the United States.

By eliminating the current anachronistic system of funding Social Security, and treating it as an annual line item of the federal government's budget, with a strict legal requirement that annual allocations are aligned with the nation's fiscal capacity, an unfunded Medicare and Social Security liability of $100 trillion would no

longer exist, from an accounting standpoint. Once this new retirement benefits funding methodology is adopted, the elimination of
that portion of the national debt owed to the Social Security trust
fund can be implemented, leaving the balance currently defined by
the U.S. government as the public debt as the actual national debt.

It will be essential to remove the Social Security trust fund obligations from the U.S. national debt, as the United States will be
faced with massive credit requirements in order to reconstruct its
banking and financial system, which we forecast to be in a state of
virtual collapse in the wake of the anticipated wave of bank
failures that will likely occur by 2012. Formulating a credible
strategy for recapitalization of its banks and credit markets is an
indispensable requirement for restoring America's economic
equilibrium, and creating a basis for rebuilding the credibility of
the nation's currency.

The cost of reconstituting America's banking and financial sector
will be severe, in large part due to the delay in addressing the
nation's systemic credit vulnerabilities comprehensively at the onset
of the global financial crisis in 2008. This will require the U.S.
Treasury to borrow trillions of dollars, however the steps outlined
above will create a level of fiscal balance that will enable the United
States to again access global credit markets. In addition, by adopting
the recommended policy options on budget restructuring and
revised tax methodologies, major overseas creditors, especially
China, will likely develop a strong interest in negotiating directly
with the United States the provision of direct loans, as well as
restructuring debt repayments that will facilitate the capability of
the U.S. government to comprehensively reform its banking system.

This report in an earlier chapter referred to the process
adopted by the Swedish government to address its acute banking
crisis in the 1990s. We recommend that aspects of the Swedish

model be incorporated in the U.S. to reconfigure its banking system. In particular, severely undercapitalized and insolvent banks must be closed, while those that can be salvaged are cleansed of their toxic assets and recapitalized. In all probability, a significant portion of the U.S. banking system will need to be temporarily nationalized. In time, these revitalized banks can be resold to the private sector, creating the possibility for the United States to recoup much of its investment and improve the national debt to GDP ratio in the long-term.

The UK faces dire challenges that are virtually identical to those confronting the United States. The United Kingdom is especially vulnerable to hyperinflation, in large part due to the aggressive degree of quantitative easing and debt monetization adopted by the Bank of England at an early stage in the evolution of the global economic crisis. For example, in 2009 the Bank of England purchased £175 billion in UK Treasury bonds, the equivalent of $280 billion at the prevailing exchange rate, representing 30% of all Treasury gilt auctions. This is a path that will assure a rise in bond yields, leading to an elevated level of inflationary pressures on the nation's economy.

In our view, the UK must adopt many of the same policy measures we have recommended for the United States. Inevitably, these proposed policy responses will involve painful consequences for the UK, however, the alternative is national insolvency, currency devaluation on a catastrophic scale and radical economic contraction.

One of the areas the UK must seriously review in an effort to impose fiscal discipline is the retention of its independent nuclear deterrent, currently based on submarine platforms. Estimates on the costs of renewing and replacing the current Trident system are in excess of $100 billion. While there may be valid national security reasons for the United Kingdom to maintain some form of nuclear deterrent until general nuclear disarmament is achieved, we believe that there are cost effective alternatives that should be seriously considered. One possibility we recommend that UK policymakers consider is merging the present independent nuclear forces of the United Kingdom and France. We believe this is a viable approach, as both nations, allies and NATO members, share common and significant long-term economic and fiscal challenges. A joint UK-French nuclear deterrent would achieve the common national security objectives of the two countries, while effectively cutting in half the vast budgetary allocations required for maintaining this strategic capability.

While the United States and UK are most directly threatened by insolvent public finances, the massive structural deficits that have occurred throughout the Euozone, as well as in Japan, Canada and Australia since the onset of the global economic crisis, augment the forces driving the sovereign debt explosion. If virtually all major advanced economies continue to run massive government deficits, this will inevitably lead to bond yield inflation. Mounting interest rates will perpetuate deficit financing by sovereigns, with a growing proportion of tax revenue being diverted towards debt interest servicing. Nations that cannot fund mounting interest rates on the international credit market will engage in debt monetization, contributing to global financial instability as well as national inflation. All these factors would mitigate against a rapid recovery from the projected synchronized global depression. Contrary to conventional Keynesian economic theory, we believe the restoration of fiscal discipline by sovereigns is an inseparable component of an effective strategy for ending the global depression.

The impending collapse of the U.S. dollar will accelerate the process of constructing a new international reserve currency or monetary unit. Even if the United States adopts the recommendations in this report, and restores functional viability to its currency, a process that will likely take several years, it is our assessment that once the U.S. dollar has lost its status as the primary international reserve currency, this displacement will be permanent.

Speculation and investigation into what will ultimately replace the American greenback as the world's universal monetary instrument has been ongoing since the liquidation of Lehman Brokers and the grave deterioration in the fiscal posture of the U.S. federal government. Various recommendations have surfaced, many involving a basket of primary currencies, including the Special Drawing Rights (SDR) established under the auspices of the IMF, which involves a formula that incorporates variable currency weights and their exchange rates over a specified and preceding period of time. Undoubtedly, proposals from circles that favor a return to the gold standard, or a global currency based on backing by precious metals, will be advanced. What must be affirmed in this report is that a transparent and durable universal mode of currency transaction must be designed and institutionalized at an early point, once the global economic crisis has transmuted into a depression. Delaying this essential requirement will extend the duration of the global economic contraction, primarily by stifling the recovery of international trade and credit markets. An effective replacement for the U.S. dollar will be an important signpost on the road to global economic recovery. Conversely, a prolonged vacuum following the downfall of the U.S. dollar will prove an impediment to all other policy actions aimed at reviving global economic activity.

Even if most of the policies and remedies we have proposed are adopted by the world's leading economic actors, the international community will be unable to avoid a period of austerity and social pain that will endure for several years. In the event that the countries most impacted by the sovereign debt crisis and its aftermath make different choices from those we recommend, we forecast grave national and geopolitical consequences. The United States is especially vulnerable to these societal and political ramifications.

Based on historical precedent, a synchronized global depression will lead to sharply elevated crime rates throughout the world. The United States, due to its weak social safety net and proliferation of private gun ownership, will witness a crime wave of massive proportions, especially involving armed robbery, kidnapping and homicides. This uncontained growth in violent criminality will undoubtedly weaken social cohesion in the United States, inflicting further damage on the national economy. Businesses that remain in operation in the U.S. will be compelled to divert scarce resources towards enhancing their security. An insolvent government, be it at the local, county, state or federal level, will be hard pressed to add additional policing and incarceration capacity to cope with the projected elevation in criminal activity.

We believe that major enterprises, especially multinational corporations, will need to design and implement cost-effective security measures to ensure the safety of employees, executives, production facilities and distribution mechanisms during what may be a protracted period of lawlessness, compounded by insolvent governments unable to maintain fully functional policing and judicial capabilities. In an environment where resources for law enforcement are diminished while simultaneously violent criminality rises dramatically, the ability to effect reliable safety and security for staff and infrastructure will be as important an element of a corporation's business plan as are those aspects addressing financial challenges.

The turbulent economic environment that will exist following the fiscal collapse of major sovereigns, in particular the U.S. and

UK, will compel businesses, both large and small, to seek alternative means of assuring supply, distribution and marketing of services and products. Improvisation will be essential, as well as advanced disaster planning. In the event that normal credit markets are utterly frozen for significant periods, other means of financing essential purchases must be defined. Stockpiling of commodities, selected production lines and other strategic inventory may become an imperative necessity, enabling businesses to engage in barter agreements. In a worst case scenario, enterprises will be compelled by the force of circumstance to find inventive ways of procuring commodities and essential goods that are required for maintaining the business. Those enterprises that fail to develop these capabilities will likely not survive the next phase of the global economic crisis.

Small business will be especially jeopardized by the projected synchronized global depression. Their most significant challenge will be severe cash flow constriction and credit contraction. Entrepreneurs operating small businesses in the brutal economic environment we foresee will lack many of the assets possessed by a large enterprise. We believe that the prospect of smaller enterprises to survive an economic depression will in large part depend on their ability to effect strategic alliances, such as cooperatives for pooling resources that include strategic inventory and highly relevant professional services. Complex mechanisms will need to be developed that can enable small business cooperatives to trade their collective assets for essential goods and services. An example might be swapping office rental for legal services, or commodities for electrical contracting. Enterprises located in the United States will be operating under particularly harsh business conditions, especially during the period when normal banking, financial and currency exchange systems are inoperative. The urgency of designing business plans incorporating the concepts and capabilities we have recommended cannot be overstated.

As major economies collapse under the burden of unsustainable public and private debt, while governments are assailed by legions of unemployed citizens, momentum for trade protectionism will accelerate. Though there is significant consensus among economic historians that protectionism in the long run inhibits economic recovery from a severe downturn on both the national and global scale, academic rationalizations are likely to become impotent when confronted by the wrath of the desperately unemployed, whose ranks will swell as the crisis worsens. On the other hand, the economic model that precipitated the global economic crisis, based in large part on exporting manufacturing and servicing jobs from advanced economies to lower wage developing nations, and accessing credit from exporting economies to finance the consumers of nations that were net importers, has proven to be hideously unbalanced and savagely flawed. In effect, a global labor arbitrage system was constructed, involving massively leveraged investments in infrastructure designed for the mass production of consumer durables, primarily for export. This worldwide chain of fabrication, packaging, shipping and delivery that involved the separation of thousands of kilometres, across continents and oceans, could only function profitably if the manufacturing mechanism is operated near peak capacity. In the severe contraction in consumer consumption that has occurred in major advanced economies, in particular the United States, this economic model has been proven to be both fragile and unsustainable.

The global economy is afflicted with massive production overcapacity, a condition that can only worsen as the worldwide recession is transformed into a synchronized depression. Unfortunately, policymakers have been obsessed with short-term remedies to a long-term problem of structural economic imbalance. A conspicuous example is the global automobile industry, which in 2009 was running at below 60% of production capacity, within the framework of facilities and suppliers spread over great geographical distances, often far removed from principle customer locations. In the face of this vexing strategic problem, decision makers in large economies have offered car scrappage schemes, such as America's "cash for clunkers," to artificially boost consumer demand for short intervals.

Confronting the fundamental structural issues that have contributed to global economic imbalances are an indispensable imperative towards resolving the global economic crisis. This would ultimately require agreement by the major advanced and developing economies on a new economic and financial architecture, a principal feature of which would be sustainable methodologies for locating the means of production and distribution as they relate to major markets. In the case of major exporters to nations that suffer from chronic international trade deficits, this will require shifting some of the production facilities to those nations. China, in particular, would be serving its long term economic interests, and forestalling a wave of domestic protectionism, by building production facilities in the United States to supply its American market. A successful precedent for this policy measure is the case of major Japanese automobile manufacturers, including Toyota and Honda, which have established a significant manufacturing presence in the U.S. and are perceived as important sources of industrial employment in that country.

The duration and severity of the global economic crisis defines a disaster that is entirely man-made. The human authors of this global catastrophe have been, in large part, driven by reckless greed and a myopic internalization of what constitutes economic self-interest. Perverse incentives enabled the upper echelons of financial enterprises to act in a manner that satisfied short-term and personal monetary interests, while sacrificing the long-term economic well-being of society as a whole. In many countries, especially the United States, a high level of political corruption facilitated this level of irresponsible behavior. The U.S. political system, in its current form, is fatally vulnerable to the influence of money in the form of campaign contributions and outright bribes. The financial and banking industry has been the major force in Washington lobbying government to adopt an agenda of market fundamentalism and radical deregulation of the financial industry. The outcome that has arisen from this unholy admixture has been a scale of human disaster that is unique in history.

Unless sovereigns are prepared to accord high-level financial criminality that imposes massive collective economic damage on the nation the same level of sanction as high treason in wartime, there will exist no effective deterrent to future episodes of such destructive behavior. Yet, no act of treason on behalf of a hostile power could have inflicted the scale of human misery and economic devastation that has been imposed by the architects of the global economic crisis. In an environment where the most culpable actors in this immense financial and economic cataclysm are bailed out by taxpayers on a scale that guarantees national insolvency, rather than being driven out of business and facing maximum legal sanction, it is clear that no deterrent to a repetition of such behavior exists. It is futile to talk about repairing the damage to the global economy without enacting the legal ordinances that alone can ensure that such a human disaster does not recur.

A final point that must be raised is the observation that has surfaced among several commentators that warfare provides a solution to a nation's severe economic problems. Some have pointed to World

War II, which is attributed by several scholars to have been the ultimate factor that ended the Great Depression in the United States.

This observation is both egregiously superficial and contextually false. History knows many examples where a political echelon that felt powerless in the face of a severe economic downturn resorted to a military conflict as a means to distract the population from its state of economic misery. In the 1930s, Germany initiated a massive military build-up in support of plans for aggressive war, while Japan waged a brutal war for new markets in China, as the solution to the economic crisis that had afflicted their societies in the wake of the Great Depression. By 1945, both nations were reduced to smouldering ruins and economic morbidity.

In a best case scenario, the global economic crisis will have subtracted tens of trillions of dollars in output and wealth from the peak potential of the world's economy. However, long-term stability in relations between the major powers and a reduction in global spending on armaments will contribute significantly towards recovery.

In the event that political leadership lacks foresight and succumbs to the most primitive instincts of national chauvinism, a new dark age of militarism and major-power rivalry is inevitable. In a world haunted by nuclear proliferation, this path will add immeasurably to the level of human misery already created by the worst economic crisis since the Great Depression. If the world's major advanced and developing economies fail to learn from the mistakes made during the last major global economic and financial crisis, far more will be at stake than the issue of economic recovery. To repeat the follies of the past, this time armed with weapons of mass destruction, will be to prove for all time that wars do not stimulate economies, but destroy them and their societies.

· CPSIA information can be obtained at www.ICGtesting.com
Printed in the USA
LVOW071746170212

269206LV00015B/103/P